TEXTBOOK OF PALAEOBOTANY

TEXTBOOK
OF
PALAEOBOTANY

By

Dr. Shubhrata R. Mishra

Dept. of Botany

Vikram University

Ujjain (M.P.)

(India)

D P H

DISCOVERY PUBLISHING HOUSE PVT. LTD.

NEW DELHI-110 002

Published by:
Namit Wasan
DISCOVERY PUBLISHING HOUSE PVT. LTD.
4383/4B, Ansari Road, Darya Ganj
New Delhi-110 002 (India)
Phone : +91-11-23279245; 23253475; 43596065
E-mail : discoverybooksindia@gmail.com
discoverypublishinghouse@gmail.com
namitwasan9@gmail.com
web : www.discoverypublishinggroup.com

***First Edition:* 2010**

***Reprinted:* 2018**

ISBN: 978-81-8356-556-1

Textbook of Palaeobotany

Printed at:
Infinity Imaging Systems
Delhi

Preface

Paleobotany is important in the reconstruction of ancient ecological systems and climate, known as paleoecology and paleoclimatology respectively; and is fundamental to the study of green plant development and evolution. Paleobotany has also become important to the field of archaeology, primarily for the use of phytoliths in relative dating and in paleoethnobotany.

Macroscopic remains of true vascular plants are first found in the fossil record during the Silurian Period of the Paleozoic era. Some dispersed, fragmentary fossils of disputed affinity, primarily spores and cuticles, have been found in rocks from the Ordovician Period in Oman, and are thought to derive from liverwort- or moss-grade fossil plants. Plant-derived macrofossils become abundant in the Late Devonian and include tree trunks, fronds, and roots. The earliest tree is Archaeopteris, which bears simple, fern-like leaves spirally arranged on branches atop a conifer-like trunk.

Fossils of plants are very different from the fossils of animals, and this is in part a result of the different architecture of plants. Animals develop with specific parts, and in both the young and adult animal, those parts exist in fixed numbers and locations. Even animals which undergo metamorphosis have only one head, and will emerge with a fixed body structure. By contrast, plants are continually producing new branches, leaves, and other parts throughout their lives. These parts may fall off without injuring the plant. Thus, plants fossils are often fragmentary pieces such as leaves, branches, or pollen.

Since a leaf, stem, spore, or seed may be found preserved without any physical connection to the plant from which it came, paleobotanists use form taxa (singular form taxon) to name and classify such fossils. When the true identity of such fossils is later discovered, the two form taxa may be merged. For example, in the 1960s fossil leaves called Archaeopteris (literally "ancient fern") were found attached to fossil wood of the tree Callixylon. The whole plant is now known to be a Devonian tree with fern-like leaves but with gymnosperm-like wood. Some form taxa continue to exist even after their identity is determined. This is a matter of convenience for identifying quickly which part was found as a fossil, especially which the fossil may come from more than one kind of plant.

—Author

Contents

1

Introduction

INTRODUCTION

Paleobotany, also spelled as palaeobotany (from the Greek words *paleon* = old and *botany*, study of plants), is the branch of paleontology or paleobiology dealing with the recovery and identification of plant remains from geological contexts, and their use for the biological reconstruction of past environments, and the evolution of both the plant kingdom and life in general. A synonym is paleophytology. Paleobotany includes the study of terrestrial plant fossils, as well as the study of prehistoric marine photoautotrophs, such as photosynthetic algae, seaweeds or kelp. A closely-related field is palynology, which is the study of fossilized and extant spores and pollen.

Paleobotany is important in the reconstruction of ancient ecological systems and climate, known as paleoecology and paleoclimatology respectively; and is fundamental to the study of green plant development and evolution. Paleobotany has also become important to the field of archaeology, primarily for the use of phytoliths in relative dating and in paleoethnobotany.

OVERVIEW OF THE PALEOBOTANICAL RECORD

Macroscopic remains of true vascular plants are first found in the fossil record during the Silurian Period of the Paleozoic era. Some dispersed, fragmentary fossils of disputed affinity, primarily spores and cuticles, have been found in rocks from the Ordovician Period in Oman, and are thought to derive from liverwort- or moss-grade fossil plants.

An important early land plant fossil locality is the Rhynie Chert, an Early Devonian sinter (hot spring) deposit composed primarily of silica found outside the town of Rhynie in Scotland. The Rhynie Chert is exceptional due to its preservation of several different clades of plants, from mosses and lycopods to more unusual, problematic forms. Many fossil animals, including arthropods and arachnids, are also found in the Rhynie Chert, and it offers a unique window on the history of early terrestrial life.

Plant-derived macrofossils become abundant in the Late Devonian and include tree trunks, fronds, and roots. The earliest tree is Archaeopteris, which bears simple, fern-like leaves spirally arranged on branches atop a conifer-like trunk. Widespread coal swamp deposits across North America and Europe during the Carboniferous Period contain a wealth of fossils containing arborescent lycopods up to 30 meters tall, abundant seed plants, such as conifers and seed ferns, and countless smaller, herbaceous plants. Angiosperms (flowering plants) evolved during the Mesozoic, and flowering plant pollen and leaves first appear during the Early Cretaceous, approximately 130 million years ago.

PLANT FOSSILS

A plant fossil is any preserved part of a plant that has long since died. Such fossils may be prehistoric impressions that are many millions of years old, or bits of charcoal that are only a few hundred years old. Prehistoric plants are various groups of plants that lived before recorded history (before about 3500 BC).

Kinds of Plant Fossils

One of the most common kinds of plant fossils is a compression fossil, in which a leaf or flattened part of the plant has been pressed between layers of sediment and often preserved as a carbonaceous film. Also common are fossil pollen and spores from ancient lake beds, as well as charcoal. Less common, but economically more important, is coal from the plants of Carboniferous swamps. One of the most spectacular of plant fossils is petrified wood.

Form Taxa

Fossils of plants are very different from the fossils of animals, and this is in part a result of the different architecture of plants. Animals develop with specific parts, and in both the young and adult animal, those parts exist in fixed numbers and locations. Even animals which undergo metamorphosis have only one head, and will emerge with a fixed body structure. By contrast, plants are continually producing new branches, leaves, and other parts throughout their lives. These parts may fall off without injuring the plant. Thus, plants fossils are often fragmentary pieces such as leaves, branches, or pollen.

Since a leaf, stem, spore, or seed may be found preserved without any physical connection to the plant from which it came, paleobotanists use form taxa (singular form taxon) to name and classify such fossils. When the true identity of such fossils is later discovered, the two form taxa may be merged. For example, in the 1960s fossil leaves called Archaeopteris (literally "ancient fern") were found attached to fossil wood of the tree Callixylon. The whole plant is now known to be a Devonian tree with fern-like leaves but with gymnosperm-like wood.

Some form taxa continue to exist even after their identity is determined. This is a matter of convenience for identifying quickly which part was found as a fossil, especially which the fossil may come from more than one kind of plant. Leaves assigned to the form taxon Sphenopteris come from both ferns and from seed plants; it usually is not possible to determine from isolated fossils which group the leaves belong to.

Some plants have remained remarkedly unchanged throughout earth's geological time scale. Early ferns had developed by the Mississippian, conifers by the Pennsylvanian. Some plants of prehistory are the same ones around today and are thus living fossils, such as *Ginkgo biloba* and *Sciadopitys verticillata*. Other plants have changed radically, or have gone extinct entirely.

A few examples of prehistoric plants are:

- Araucaria mirabilis;
- Archaeopteris;

- Calamites;
- Cycads;
- Glossopteris;
- Horsetails;
- Hymenaea protera; and
- Protosalvinia.

Although most of the "green things" that populate our oceans and continents don't have the ability to move about and, hence, grab out attention, the world's biota couldn't exist without these organisms. The Plant Kingdom is the base of earth's food chain and, as such, is the foundation for all life as we know it today, in the recent past, and in the deep past. That's not to say that today's biota is exactly like that of the past. Indeed, there have been dramatic changes in the base of the food chain since its first appearance. Documentation of these changes and understanding the reasons for these changes is only part of what Paleobotany — the study of fossil plants sensu latu (in the broad sense) — attempts to do.

Those scientists who actively pursue study of these seemingly "uninteresting" organisms have devised several approaches to examine life's history that can be separated into two broad categories: traditional and integrative approaches. Traditional approaches follow methodologies established during and immediately after the Renaissance, while Integrative approaches are based upon methodologies that could only be established following advances in technology of the 20th Century. Advances in analytical techniques in the next several decades will, once again, change the way in which we approach this and other disciplines but, the traditional approaches will remain basic to all avenues of research. If you don't know how it was preserved, what it is, how it is constructed, and what is its life cycle, you can't take the organism(s) and use it with any amount of credibility for more synthetic approaches in our desire to develop local, regional, and global models of how Earth works. Traditional approaches to studying plant fossils include the following:

Systematics - The attempt at a natural classification of plants. If we consider organisms that are capable of photosynthesis as being inclusive within the "Plant Kingdom," then there is a wide variety of organisms that can be accommodated in this category. These include organisms that belong to the Monera (Cyanobacteria & Bacteria); Protista (Slime molds, Brown Algae, Red Algae, Diatoms & Golden Brown Algae, Yellow-Green Algae, Dinoflagellates, Euglenoids, Grass-green Algae); and Plantae (Bryophyta, Tracheophyta). Additionally, decomposers in the Fungi are included within paleobotanical studies.

Morphology - The way in which plants are constructed. Roots, stems, photosynthetic appendages, and reproductive structures are all considered under this approach.

Anatomy and Histology - The recognition and delimitation of plant cells, tissues and organs.

Evolution and Diversification - The changes in plant types and increase in biodiversity and complexity of different plant groups through time as a function of genetic processes (interbreeding, mutation, etc.).

Coal Geology - The role in which plants contribute to the stored potential energy of the Carbon Cycle.

Integrative approaches, developed within the past half-century, include:

Whole Plant Paleobiology - The incorporation of all aspects of a plant's vegetative and reproductive parts to understand its role in the plant kingdom.

Paleoecology and Ecosystem Dynamics - Plants interact with their environment and are the basis of the ecosystem. These interactions are discernible in the fossil record and allow paleobotanists to compare them to present ecosystems to assess the evolution of the community through time.

Paleobiogeography - This involves the distribution of plant communities globally through time and their changes in distribution as it relates to both geological and climatological influences.

Paleoclimatology - Terrestrial plants are the most sensitive organisms to changes in climate on the continental scale. The distribution of major vegetational and forest types provides the best assessment of global climate change that has affected emergent land surfaces, and provides an independent test of models developed from oceanic data sets or computer simulations.

Taphonomy - The processes responsible for the development, burial, and preservation of plant parts not only as fossils but also as Organic Carbon. This involves an understanding of sedimentology and sedimentary processes.

Energy Resources and Organic Geochemistry - The incorporation of plant-derived Organic Carbon has been demonstrated to be in integral part of all hydrocarbon-forming environments (petroleum & natural gas).

Evolutionary Mechanisms - Plants provide independent tests of hypotheses concerning the mechanisms responsible for and acting upon organic evolution. Multi-variate mathematical techniques have been developed to assess inter-relationships of character states (morphological and anatomical features) that allow for hypothesis testing.

A Systematic Functional Morphology - Plant organization appears to be independent of systematic affinity, and specific adaptations evolve in response to specific conditions. Assessment of such morphologies provides evidence for organic "problem solving".

There is a whole lot more to the study of fossil plants than what is imagined by the general public. Paleobotany can be a dynamic and contributing science to a working knowledge of biological systems of the past, present, and possibly the future.

Cooksonia

The first fossils of macroscopic land plants have been found in the Middle Silurian of Ireland. They are about 425 million years old. They consist of small bifurcations some centimeters in size. Only in the very last part of the Silurian fossils of land-plants become more common and also more complete. The best known plant from that time is called Cooksonia. It is named after Isabel Cookson, who occupied herself with intensive collecting and describing plantfossils.

The little plant looked very simple: a stem which bifurcated a couple of times topped with small spheres in which the spores were formed. Thus sporangia. No leaves, no flowers, no seeds. And roots? Probably horizontal growing stems, connected with the soil by root hairs, took the function of roots. But this is not sure for fossils proving this have not been found yet.

During many millions of years it was mainly this kind of plants that grew on humid places on the land. The evolution from algae to land plants must have been a lengthy process. Many conditions had to be fulfilled before plants were able to maintain themselves on the land. There is at first the everlasting danger of desiccation. The remedy which developed is a thin waxy layer at the surface of the plant: the cuticle. Generally algae don't have a cuticle, nearly all land plants do.

But a land plant also has to breath and it needs the possibility to assimilate carbondioxide from the air to generate its nutriments. Thus the isolation by the cuticle can not be absolute. That's why the stomata have evolved, which can be opened and closed if necessary. Another problem for land plants is that they miss the upward force of the water. To be able to keep upright supporting tissue is needed. Already in Cooksonia xylem vessels have been recorded. These are vessels with annular or spiral shaped thickenings at the walls, which give them solidity. Through these vessels water is transported from the soil to the plant cells.

Another important adaptation to landlife is the very tough wall that evolved around the spores. This provided the spores with an excellent protection against desiccation, fungi, and so on. In fact they became nearly invulnerable, for they have been fossilised very often. Species of Cooksonia are found at several places on earth, e.g. in Wales, Scotland, England, Czechia and Canada. The finding of a fairly complete plant is a rare occurrence. I was already very glad with the bifurcated little stem with two sporangia between Cooksonia-chaff on the photo. Cooksonia has become extinct in the Early Devonian.

Baragwanathia

A plant, almost as old as Cooksonia, is *Baragwanathia longifolia*. There has been a lot of discussion about the age of this clubmoss-like plant, but now it is believed to be Early Ludlow (from 420 million years on). The repeatedly branched stems have a length of 10 to 20 cm and they are covered with long, needle-like leaves. Sometimes sporangia are present and transverse sections of the stems show a vascular strand like in other higher plants. The plant has a remarkably high degree of development in relation to its age. *Baragwanathia longifolia* has only been found in Australia.

Enigmatic Plants

At the time of the first Cooksonias a completely different group of plants has evolved, which tried to colonize the land. These plants are still enigmatic for scientists. Research for the real nature and the ecology of these plants is still in full progress. We shall mention three of them (there are more): Nematothallus, Parka and Pachytheca.

Fossils of Nematothallus look like black patches measuring 0,5 to 6 cm. They are irregular in shape and sometimes there is still a thick cuticle on the plant. It is possible to make a microscopic preparation of a piece of cuticle and in some cases it turns out to have a cell structure. As this has not developed in the way of cell division in higher plants it is called pseudo cell structure. Under the cuticle is a little mat consisting of very thin threads or tubes. The diameter of such a tube varies from 3 μm to 40 μm (1 μm = one thousandst of a millimeter). Spores have also been found in the mats. Apparently Nematothallus did consist of a thallus of fine threads (Gr. *nemato* = thread) covered by a thick cuticle, sometimes with a pseudo cell structure. Plants like these do not exist any more, however there are recent lichens resembling Nematothallus in several aspects. Fossils of Nematothallus have been found in formations from the Middle Silurian up to and including the Early Devonian. In Great-Britain they are found in several places.

A second enigmatic plant is Parka. This is a flat, circular to irregular patch covered by discs about 2 mm wide. These are sporangia each containing some 35,000 spores. The diameter of this plant varies from 0,5 cm to 7 cm. Where the sporangia have disappeared from the fossils, and this is often the case, a kind of reticulum remains. For a long time Parka has been supposed to be a collection of some animal's eggs. Especially in the region of Forfar, north of Dundee in Scotland, Parka is very common.

The third still unelucidated plant is Pachytheca. This fossil resembles a gleaming little globe with a diameter between 1 and 7 mm. In transverse the sphere has an outer layer with radial tubes and a nucleus in which the tubes are going in all directions. For a long time Pachytheca was thought to be part of a bigger plant, but nowadays it is firmly believed to be a complete organism. The fossils have been found in e.g. Belgium and Great-Britain. This plant too became extinct in the Early Devonian.

Probably these and similar alga-like plants can be considered as an evolutionary experiment to colonize the land. It seems having been a dead end. It is not unlikely that these plants have lost the increasing competition with the succesful higher plants.

2

The Evolution of Plants

INTRODUCTION

The oldest fossils of land plants visible with the naked eye are about 425 million years old. They are miniscule plants from the Mid-Silurian of Ireland en are called 'Cooksonia'. Cooksonia plants had dichotomously divided little stems with small knobs at the end. These knobs were sporangia and they were filled with spores. During about 20 or 30 millions of years these were the most common plants. They became extinct at the end of the Early Devonian. In the photo on the left my finest specimen of Cooksonia. It comes from South Wales and measures 3.5 cm.

The microscopic remains have been found in Oman indicating that land plants existed already 475 million years ago. Probably land plants have developed from green algae living in the sea. During the Early Devonian, from about 410 million years ago, more variation came into the flora. New groups of plants came into existence, but still the plants were small (up to 50 cm). Flowers developed only 250 millions of years later. Leaves didn't exist either, except for the scalelike leaves, like those of the clubmosses.

Several plants had spines. These were not for defending the plant, for animal life on the land was still minimal and the land animals were very small (millipedes, collembolans, trigonotarbids ('spiders'), very small crustaceans, etc.). Probably the function of the spines was to enlarge the green surface and so to enhance the assimilation. Furthermore the spines could have given more hold to the plants in forming small bushes of plants of the same species, hanging more or less on each other. All plants of that period were cryptogams (plants with spores), like at present the mosses, the ferns, the clubmosses and the horsetails. But they are so different from the living plants, that in nearly all cases it is impossible to identify to which group of recent plants they belong. All those ancient plants have become extinct.

Relatively little is known about these primitive plants, because only a small number of complete and well preserved plants have been found. In most cases the plants have been transported by rivers before they ended up in the mud and could fossilize. Therefore the plants were mostly cut to small pieces before getting fossil. There are only a limited number of places where plants from the Silurian, the Lower and Middle Devonian have been well preserved. A huge source of information on the oldest land plants is the so called 'Rhynie chert'.

About 400 million years ago there was a kind of Yellowstone Park near the place where Rhynie is now situated. There were erupting vulcanos and geysers belching boiling water, saturated with silicium. That is how a complete silicified marsh came into existence with exceptionally well preserved plants, even showing their cell structure. Many animals have also been found in the chert.

During the Middle Devonian the plants became taller and little trees arose, sized up to a couple of meters. Recently a trunk with attached crown has been discovered in the State of New York. This tree is called Eospermatopteris and it could be sized up to 8 m. It lived in the late Middle Devonian. Read more about this subject.

From the Late Devonian, Archaeopteris (don't confuse it with the ancient bird Archaeopterix) is the most well-known tree. It was possibly a predecessor of the conifers and this tree could reach a height of 18 m. The drawing on the left is a reconstruction from the fine website Devonian Times. Especially in Belgium quite a number of plants from the Upper Devonian are found. An example is Rhacophyton, occurring in the region of Liège, which could very well be a precursor of the ferns. It lacks still leaves, but it has small hooks at the end of the branches.

At the end of the Devonian the first plants with seeds came into being. The oldest seed plant of Europe has been found in Belgium and it is has got its name after the village of Moresnet: (Moresnetia). This plant has primitive seeds: they are not yet entirely enveloped, like modern seeds. Recently, a precursor of this plant has been discovered in Belgium with still more primitive 'seeds'.

The seed plants have become more and more important in the course of the hundreds of million years. It appeared to be a successful formula because now-a-days by far most plants are seed plants. The free-sporing plants have been pushed into the background.

About 450 million years ago, at the end of the Ordovician and in the beginning of the Silurian, the land was desolate and empty. Barren, hardly wethered rockgrounds, empty sand-, gravel- and clayplains, no green. Maybe some lichens. And at wet spots some algae with a couple of spider-like little creatures creeping around. In the neighbourhood of the mouth of rivers, where the water regularly flooded the land, it was probably green with algae. At such places, e.g. in Australia, traces of big seascorpions have been found. There was not much happening on the land. Life enacted itself nearly completely in the water.

The oldest indications for the existence of real land plants have been found in cores from boreholes in Oman. They contained fours of mutually connected spores (tetrads) enveloped by remains of the spore sac in which they had been formed. Research on the spore walls point to a relationship with the liverworts. The fossils have been found in the Middle Ordovician and are about 475 million years old.

SPINY PLANTS

During the Early Devonian (405 - 385 million years ago) several other groups of plants developed. They had the common feature of being rather small (not higher than half a meter) and simply structured.

Thus the plant Sawdonia ornata had no leaves, but it did have spines. The function of the spines was probably to enlarge the surface for the assimilation of carbon dioxide from the air. They were not needed for defense for the first vertebrate land animals (the amphibians) did not appear before the Middle Devonian. Possibly the plants formed thick shrubberies using the spines as a hold.

Another spiny plant from the Early Devonian is Drepanophycus spinaeformis. This one had a thicker stem with firm spiny leaves. The stems are often found without the spines. In this case the scars will be visible.

The compressed fossils of Devonian plants scarcely give any information. Determining these very old plants is extremely difficult as hardly anything shows on the fossils. Only stems, bifurcations and possibly spines. With luck you find sporangia. In that case it might be possible to detect the name of the plant. Sometimes the cuticle has stayed intact. After chemical treatment it is possible to make a microscope preparation of it in which e.g. cells an stomata are visible.

RHYNIE CHERT

The discovery of a silicified moor near the Scottish village of Rhynie, 40 km north-east of Aberdeen, has revealed a lot about the structure of very old plants. About 400 million years ago, in the beginning of the Devonian, there was a kind of Yellowstone park with vulcanos and geysers at that location. Some of the geysers spouted boiling, siliceous water with intervals of a couple of years which caused the vegetation, including the underlying peat layers, to silicify. The fossils in this so called Rhynie Chert are so perfect that the plants can be studied within the accuracy of cell structure level. It is possible to make very thin slices of the fossil bearing chert, which can be viewed under the microscope. The Rhynie Chert was discovered in 1912 by the geologist Dr. W. Mackie. The paleobotanists R. Kidston and W.H. Lang have published a very extensive description of the plants and the fungi in the chert from 1917 to 1922. In the last decades many new discoveries have been made.

The diameter of the stem is in reality 1, 3 mm. By clicking Rhynia is very close to the primeval plant from which most of the modern plants have originated. A second plant common in the Rhynie Chert is called Asteroxylon. It is a very early member of the clubmoss group. In the picture you can see the wood vessels of this plant, reinforced with annular and spiral thickenings. Of a third plant, Horneophyton, the sporangia and the spores are found often. Typical of higher plants is that the spores are formed in clusters of four. For some time these often cluster in so called tetrads. Click the photo to see one. One spore has a diameter of about 50 µm. The Rhynie Chert is also full of fungal hyphae (threads) and spores. This means that already in the Early Devonian plant remains decomposed by fungal activity. Further many little animals have been found. Mostly they are under 1 mm. In most cases it concerns mites and springtails. At the moment research is still in full progress. The Rhynie Chert is of equal importance for the understanding of the oldest land plants as the Burgess Shale for animal life. (click here for more photos of the plants and animals of the Rhynie chert).

FURTHER DEVELOPMENTS

From the Early Devonian the flora evolution gains momentum. Wereas the number of species in the Late Silurian could be counted on the fingers of two hands, in the Early Devonian this has become quite impossible. Yet at that moment the number of species was still very limited and in many cases the vegetation at a certain spot consisted of only one species or a very small number of species. At the rare finding places of well-preserved Early Devonian plant fossils one often tends to find one dominating species with the occasional sparse occurrence of other species.

The plants still have a relatively simple structure, like Zosterophyllum from the Forfar area in Scotland. This plant lacks leaves: gas exchange was entirely through the stems. The ultimate branchings of the twigs are coiled up in spirals, a feature occurring in many primitive plants. The sporangia are placed in long, loose spikes. Some stems of Zosterophyllum are found showing K- or H-like branching. These are probably underground stems (rhizomes). Another plant from the Zosterophyllum group is Gosslingia from the Brecon Beacons in Wales. This one is slightly younger than the plants of the Rhynie Chert.

The further the Devonian proceeds, the more forms appear and the higher some plant species become. In the Middle Devonian tree 'ferns' appear with a height of some meters. In the Late Devonian some plant groups develop the ability to form thicker stems by means of secundary development. Thus we see the appearance of woody stems enabling the plants to form trees. In the Late Devonian there are already rather high trees up to 8 meters.

During the Middle and the Late Devonian more species with leaves or leaflike structures appear. These developed through 'webbing' of finely branched twigs, i.e. the twigs became connected by intervening tissue. In the fernlike plant Rhacophyton from the Belgian Late Devonian this is not yet the case. However the branches in a way resemble fern leaves. The sporangia of this plant are growing in clusters with a diameter of about 2.5 cm.

SEED PLANTS

The oldest seed plants date from the Late Devonian. The special feature of seeds is their being enveloped. In Moresnetia (so called after the town of Moresnet in Belgium) this envelope is not yet completely closed. It is placed around the seed like a sort of calyx, leaving the top of the seed visible. Moresnetia is one of the oldest seed plants in the world and the oldest in Europe. For the time being, for new discoveries are made regularly. In Belgium extraordinary well preserved specimens have been found, in which even the seeds are visible.

The oldest seed plants were gymnosperms for the seeds were not yet embedded in an ovary. From this kind of plants the many species of seed ferns developed that grew in the coalswamps during the Carboniferous. And a Moresnetia-like plant must have been the ancestor of all modern flowering plants. Surely a plant to treat with respect.

3

Cooksonia

INTRODUCTION

The evolution of the first land plants was a major event in the history of Earth. It cleared the way for the irresistible development of animal life on the land. And it was the land plants which changed the biosphere thoroughly, e.g. the oxygen rate, the carbonic acid rate, the soil structure and the character of the erosion. The most famous Silurian land plant is a small creature sized up to a couple of centimeters, named Cooksonia. It is not only the best-known plant, but up to now also the oldest one. Yet a lot is unknown about it. For example the way in which the plant was attached to the soil. Finding Cooksonia-fossils is difficult because only a few occurrences are known (marine, delta of river deposits from the Late Silurian and the earliest Devonian). The small size of the plant is also a disadvantage for finding. A rather complete plant is very rare.

SPECIES

W.H. Lang published the first species of Cooksonia in 1937: *C. pertoni* en *C. hemisphaerica*. He used Lower Devonian specimens from Wales for his description. They were a few centimeters high, one or more times dichotomously branched and they were bearing more or less globose sporangia at the end of the branches. Leaves and other appendices were absent. He gave the genus name Cooksonia in honour of the Australian paleobotanist Isabel Cookson with whom he co-operated in the research of the likewise very old plant Baragwanathia from Australia. Since then there are reports of Cooksonia-species from places all over the world: Wales, Scotland, England, Bohemia, Kazakhstan, Siberia, de state of New York, Canada, China, Bolivia and Brazil. The best-known species are *C. pertoni, C. hemisphaerica, C. cambrensis, C. caledonica,* all described on the basis of British fossils. Furthermore recently the new species *C. paranensis* from Brazil has been described.

The species are characterized by the shape of the sporangia and the subtending axis. Because of the variability of the form of the sporangia identification of the species is often difficult or even impossible. The angle with the layer in which the sporangium has been preserved is also of great influence on the shape of the fossil. Therefore it is important for identification to have several sporangia at one's disposal.

Cooksonia-sporangia did not have an special adaptation for dehiscence at maturity. Probably the sporangium simply tore open at the upper side.

Cooksonia-species

Cooksonia pertoni. The sporangia of this plant are much broader than high. They are often so flat that they look plate-shaped. The subtending stalk is strongly widening, whereby the bearing part is nearly as wide as the sporangium. The sporangium is not sunken into the axis.

Cooksonia hemisphaerica. The shape of the sporangia is semiglobose, globose or elliptical. The stalk is widening below the sporangium and the sporangium is at most about three times as wide as the top of the stalk.

Sporangia close to the bifurcation are mostly nicely round, while sporangia at longer stalks are more irregularly shaped. The sporangia at short stalks are likely to be younger.

Cooksonia cambrensis. The plant bears globose or elliptical sporangia, sitting on stalks which are not or hardly thickening below the sporangium. The difference with *C. hemisphaerica* is that the axis of *C. cambrensis* is relatively much thinner immediately below the sporangium.

Cooksonia caledonica (link to other website). The sporangia are variably shaped but in most cases wider than high or even kidney-shaped. At the upper side a coaly border can be seen in some cases. The stalk is somewhat widening below the sporangium.

C. paranensis. This species has been described by P. Gerrienne *et al* in 2001 on the basis of hundreds of specimens from the Lower Devonian of Brazil. The plant has a plate-shaped or bowl-shaped sporangium, that is more or less sunken within the axis. Sporangium and stalk together are trumpet-shaped. The sporangium does not project like that of *C. pertoni*.

Cooksonia must be seen as an artificial genus. It probably consists of several genera, which cannot be distinguished at the moment. The presence of xylem vessels with annular or spiral-shaped thickenings at the walls counts as characteristic for higher plants. Algae and mosses do not have such tracheids. Several stems of Cooksonia show a central black line or thickening, which is probably the remainder of a xylem strand.

Yet there are several snags in the assumption that every plant of Cooksonia had tracheids. In the first place no tracheids have been found in Silurian Cooksonia fossils. So it is possible that the tracheids developed only in the course of time.

Secondly it has been discovered with the use of electron microscopy that in different species of Lower Devonian plants two kinds of strengthened 'xylem' strands occurred. One of those appears to be related to the central strands of mosses.

Tentatively it is assumed that the oldest Cooksonia's were also in the possession of tracheids.

Spores

In most cases no spores are present in the sporangia. Sometimes they have been preserved, but as a heavily compressed mass in which the individual spores can hardly be distinguised. Only very seldom have they been preserved in a rather good, threedimensional form. On the right hand side a drawing after a SEM-photo of a spore of C. pertoni (diameter 30μms.

Research on spores of C. *pertoni* from different places in Great Britain has revealed an evolutionary trend. The existence of four different types of spores in C. *pertoni* has been proved: two are common and two rare. There appears to be a tendency from smooth spores in the Silurian to more ornamented ones in the Early Devonian. Of course the advantage of ornamented spores for the plant remains uncertain, but it could possibly be an adaptation to drought. Comparable smooth spores have been found in the Lower Silurian. Though the oldest known Cooksonia-fossils are of Mid-Silurian age, this could point to an even earlier occurrence of Cooksonia or other plants.

OCCURRENCES

The oldest Cooksonia-fossils have been found in Ireland. They date from the Late-Wenlock (425 million years). The preservation is not good enough to identify them at species name, but they are clearly Cooksonia-like plants with sporangia. Axes without sporangia are also found, some of them with up to three branchings. Somewhat younger Cooksonia-fossils have been found in North-Wales, at a locality in the Lower Ludlow (420 million years). These fossils are diminutive. My biggest fossil from this place is a branchlet with two bifurcations measuring 15 mms. Axes like these are sometimes placed in the artificial genus Hostinella. Some of the axes show a black line, probably pointing at the presence of xylem vessels.

Silurian Cooksonia-fossils have also been found at some other places in Wales and Shropshire. Edwards even found all four from Great Britain described species at one locality on the South coast of Wales. Outside Great Britain Silurian Cooksonia-fossils have been found in Canada (not identifiable at species name) , Bolivia (resembles C. caledonica), Czech Republic (C. hemisphaerica), Kazakhstan (not identifiable), China (the same), Siberia (C. pertoni, C. hemisphaerica), the state of New York (not yet identified) and perhaps in Libya.

C. *paranenis* from Brazil is dated as uppermost Silurian or lowermost Devonian. This last find demonstrates the occurrence of Cooksonia at a considerable shale in parts of the large southern continent Gondwana.

Cooksonia also occurs in younger deposits. *C. caledonica* has been described on the basis of Lower Devonian fossils from the area around Forfar (Scotland).

River deposits from the Lower Devonian of England have yielded fragmentary, but extremely well preserved fossils of all British species of Cooksonia. Detailed studies could be made of the structure of the sporangia and the spores of these fossils.

A new species, *C. banksii*, has been described from this locality, which resembles very much the Brasilian Cooksonia.

WAY OF GROWING

It is striking that most of the sediments containing Cooksonia are marine ones. Probably the plant grew at plains along the rivers which became submerged from time to time. Stems of the plants were then broken off, transported and buried in the sediments on the bottom of the sea. This could explain why roots or horizontally growing stems (rhizomes) have never been found until now. Cooksonia was likely to have rhizomes, for another early plant, Rhynia, related to Cooksonia, was attached to the soil in that way. The horizontally growing stems of this species developed root hairs at places where the stems touched the ground. Perhaps the strange branching at the right hand side could be a rhizome. That would be a major find! Salt marshes have also been mentioned as possible growing places for Cooksonia. It is furthermore likely that the plants were growing in vegetations existing of only one species. Most of the Early Devonian plants were also living in such monospecific vegetations. The Brazilian *C. paranensis* grew in an area not far from the South Pole at that time under probably rather extreme circumstances. Though the flora indicates an ice-free environment, the sunken sporangia appear to be an adaptation to low temperatures. Cooksonia probably grew as a small shrub.

4

Pachytheca

INTRODUCTION

Sometimes small glossy spheres are found in sediments of the Upper Silurian and the Lower Devonian. They measure 1 to 6 mm and possess a characteristic internal structure. Hooker named them Pachytheca in 1853, meaning 'thick sporangium'. In the first half of the 19th century they were considered to be seedlike objects or parts of fish jaws. From 1889 on Hooker took the little spheres for algae or colonies of algae and nowadays they are also regarded as alga-like organisms.

Pachytheca is most frequently found in the countries of western Europe: Scotland, Wales, England, Belgium, France and Germany, but there are also finds from other parts of the world, like Canada and Australia.

The specimens of Lac de la Gileppe in Belgium are exceptionally well preserved. Broken specimens show a spherical inner zone, surrounded by a thick cortex. Using a lens the fibrous structure of this cortex and the radially arrangement of the fibers are visible. Dr. P. Gerrienne from Liège (Belgium) has described these Pachytheca's in detail in 1991. The SEM-photos below are from his article (with permission). The cortex consists of thin, straight tubes in which sometimes an algal thread appears. Tubes occur also in the inner zone, but these are strongly curved and run in all directions. They are in most cases poorly preserved indicating a less solid structure. This could be the reason that many specimens of Pachytheca are found with an empty or sedimentfilled inner zone. Several times a channel has been observed and there is a possibility that this channel had something to do with the, still not elucidated, reproduction of the plant.

The specimens of Lac de la Gileppe in Belgium have been so well preserved that they often show the detailed internal structure. For that purpose a peel can be made from the fossil. A piece of rock with Pachytheca in it, is sawn through and polished. The polished surface is then etched with diluted hydrochloric acid. In this way a thin layer of chalk is removed whereas the organic parts remain. After rinsing and drying aceton is poored over the etched surface and a piece of acetate folium is put over it. This is pressed to the surface and pulled off after some drying time. The organic remains are now on the peel and they can be studied under the microscope.

A short time ago Hans-Jürgen Weiss from Rabenau (Germany) has found a well preserved specimen of Pachytheca in a piece of Rhynie chert. Click here to study this fossil. Pachytheca belongs to a group of enigmatic plants, which conquered the land at about the same time as higher plants (like Cooksonia) did. Other members of this group are Nematothallus, Parka and Prototaxites. All plants of these group became extinct during the Devonian. For already as long as 150 years the Devonian fossil Prototaxites has been collected and studied, but still there is no certainty about its identity. The American J.W. Dawson, who was the first to describe it (1859), thought it was rotted wood, related to Taxus. That's why he gave it that name. At the end of the nineteenth century scientists began to think it was an alga, in fact a brown alga, and this opinion has been established and is now mentioned in nearly every book.

Until an American paleobotanist, Francis Hueber, after 20 years of research published an elaborated paper (2001) in which he defended that Prototaxites was the fruiting body of an enormous fungus. And now there is Marc-André Selosse from Paris, who proposes with good arguments that we might have to do with a huge lichen!

PROTOTAXITES

Prototaxites looks like fossil wood. It is found in the shape of trunks or parts of trunks and these always show more or less clear rings resembling annual rings of trees. On a beach in Saudi Arabia lies broken trunk measuring 5.3 m, which has a diameter of 1.37 m at the base and 1.02 m at the other end. In New York State a trunk has been found sized 8.83 m with a diameter of only 34 cm at one end and 21 cm at the other one. Dawson has described a specimen from Gaspé (Canada) with a length of 2.13 m and a maximum diameter of 91 cm. All these trunks are silicified.

In Holland Prototaxites is not rare among boulders sucked up from the rivers or found in quarries in the east of the country. These are also silicified specimens showing more or less clear (parts of) rings. Besides they are characterized by a silky surface. Most pieces are rather small, but sometimes bigger ones are found.

Prototaxites had its 'flowering' time in the Early Devonian and became extinct in the Late Devonian.

In some Lower Devonian strata in Scotland, Wales and Germany Prototaxites is found in a different kind of conservation, viz. compressed and (sometimes) carbonized. The 'stems' are often bedded together with land plants like Zosterophyllum and Pachytheca and they are striking because of their width. In this case they also resemble fossil wood, but the rings are not visible now. Obviously the trunks have fallen apart in small pieces during the transportation by the rivers. The dimensions vary from millimeters to 30 cm long and 15 cm wide.

GILEPPE

Not far from the Lac de la Gileppe near Liège in Belgium a kind of rock occurs containing very small pieces of Prototaxites. Most of these pieces are smaller than 1 cm. The robust trunks have been reduced to fragments having the size of a piece of a match by the transportation through the rivers. Very special in this sedimentation is that the inner structure of the fossil has been preserved remarkably well. The microphotos below and on the next page are taken from peels from this rock. (A peel is produced by etching a polished surface with an acid and, after washing and drying, pouring acetone over it and pressing cellulose-acetate foil on the surface. The foil can be pulled off when the acetone has dried up, taking the organic remains with it. These can be studied under the microscope).

The Inner Structure

The specimens of Prototaxites from Gaspé, which Dawson had been using in 1859 for his description and of which Hueber used one for his paper (the others have disappeared), show an exceptionally well preserved inner structure. Prototaxites doesn't have cells like land plants (and consequently wood), but it has tubes. Until some years ago two kinds of tubes were distinguished: thick ones with a diameter of 18 - 50 μm and thin ones with a diameter of 2-6 μm.

The thick tubes have a thick wall (2-6 μm), they do not branch and they are not septate. They are quite long, but because of their somewhat flexuous course they run out of the slides and that's why the maximum length is unknown. Lengths of 2.5 mm have been observed.

The thin tubes are profusely branched in all directions and tangle around the thick tubes. They are septate with a pore in the septa and have cells measuring 15-54 μm.

Hueber has described a third kind, which is less common. These are thick tubes (15-45 μm), but contrarily to the first kind they branch frequently, they are strongly curved, they have thin walls and they are septate. Furthermore there is a pore in the septa. In some places they are so profusely branched that clusters are formed, which can be seen on a polished surface as spots of a different.

Fruiting bodies of fungi have an inner structure of tubes, called hyphae. There are three types of hyphae: skeletal hyphae, binding hyphae and generative hyphae. Most fungi exist of only one of these types (the generative hyphae), but some have two or three. The skeletal hyphae are (mostly) straight, stiff and they are thickwalled. They occur in some fungi living on wood. The binding hyphae wind between the other hyphae , they have septa and, as the name says, they have a binding task. The generative hyphae have a reproductive function : they form the structures which eventually bring forth the sporeproducing cells. They are thinwalled, septate and they branch repeatedly.

It is thus quite understandable that Hueber uses these terms in his description of the structure of Prototaxites. The thick, unbranched tubes are in Hueber's view skeletal hyphae: they provided stiffness to the organism. The thin, winding tubes are binding hyphae: they held the skeletal hyphae together and contributed in this way to the toughness of the body. The thick, branching tubes with septa are generative hyphae.

A difference between Prototaxites and living fungi is the fact that the skeletal hyphae of Prototaxites are relatively much thicker: on average about 30 μm compared to 5-10 μm in the recent fungi. Binding hyphae however, both fossil and recent ones, have about the same diameter: 3 μm. The generative hyphae of Prototaxites again are much thicker than those in living fungi. Click on the middle photo below to see skeletal and binding hyphae of Fomes fometarius.

ASCOMYCETES AND BASIDIOMYCETES

The fungi can be divided into several groups. Two of these are the best-known: the Ascomycetes and the Basidiomycetes. In the first group the sexual spores are formed in elongated sac-shaped cells, in the second group they are formed on the top of minute projections growing from special cells, called basidia. These sac-shaped cells and basidia originate from a layer of cells, called hymenium, which is formed on special parts of the fruiting body of the fungus, e.g. the gills or the pores. In the Basidiomycetes the spores are 'launched' when they have reached maturity.

Hueber has found structures in his slides resembling (incomplete) basidia and thus he assumes that Prototaxites belonged to the Basidiomycetes.

Origin of the Rings

The presence of rings in the trunks of Prototaxites can be explained by supposing that a new growth increment was formed time and again. This occurs also in living fruiting bodies of fungi. An example is the Echte Tonderzwam which shows growth increments not only on the outside but also in the inner structure.

Hueber concludes from his microscopical research that the hymenium of Prototaxites covered the whole outside of the fruiting body. This occurs in recent fungi among others in *Clavariadelphus pistillaris*. From time to time a new layer of tissue was formed on the outside mainly consisting of skeletal and binding hyphae but also with some generative hyphae. At a certain moment the generative hyphae started to branch frequently and they formed a new hymenium on the outside of the fruiting body. Such a combination of an all-covering hymenium and periodical growth increments does not occur in the living fungi, but the separate systems do (as shown before).

Medullary Spots

On polished surfaces of well-preserved American specimens of Prototaxites rather regularly spread, spindle-shaped spots can be observed, resembling mark rays in some way. I could not find them in my own specimens, probably because of the bad state of conservation. Slides prove that in these spots the generative hyphae are profusely branching, forming clusters. Hueber speaks of 'coltricioide clusters' because this kind of clusters is also found in Coltricia perennis. The different colour on these spots could be caused by mucous secretion or something like that. The spots are coloured black in the growth model above.

CLAMPS AND DOLIPORES

Characteristic for generative hyphae in recent fungi are clamps. These are formed when new cells are produced. A clamp is a bow-shaped thickening at the place of a septum in a hypha. It is beyond the purpose of this site to go deeply into this matter, but the main aspect is that the clamps are necessary for the distribution of the nuclei over the cells when a new cell is formed.

The septa in the hyphae are perforated by a small canal, called dolipore. This enables the interchange of protoplasm between the cells.

Hueber has found some clamps, or better remains of clamps, in the generative hyphae of Prototaxites.

The difference between Prototaxites and living 'woody' fungi is the unlimited perennial growth of Prototaxites. Therefore the fruiting body could grow so large. The only limitations were, according to Hueber, the capacity of the mycelium to provide enough food and water, and influences from outside, e.g. storms. Living woody fungi can also grow very large: fruiting bodies of 1 m have been observed.

Because branched specimens are hardly ever found, Hueber concludes that Prototaxites must have been the columnar fruiting body of a huge fungus, sized up to 8 m. Probably rootlike structures (rhizomorphs) served for anchoring in the ground. Click here to see the Hueber's fine reconstruction again.

Prototaxites must have been by far the greatest element in the landscape of the Early Devonian. Plants did not grow taller than around 50 cm at the time and stems did not become thicker than a couple of centimeters.

The scientists have investigated the ratio of the carbon isotopes C-12 and C-13 in Prototaxites and in plants found in the same layer. This ratio showed a much larger variation in Prototaxites than in the vascular plants. This fact can only been understood by assuming that Prototaxites did not make its own food from carbon dioxide and water but that it gained its food from the underground (like fungi do). A microbial mat with a dominance of cyanobacteria is a possible underground. Such mats were probably rather common in that time, whereas they now exist only at places where plants cannot live (e.g. stromatolites in Australia).

In 1872 the Englishman William Carruthers published a venomous comment on Dawson's opinion that Prototaxites was petrified conifer wood. He proposed three possibilities: a lichen, a fungus or an alga, but was convinced that it was an alga and he gave it a new (invalid) name: Nematophycus, meaning thread plant.

For intuitive reasons Prototaxites has mainly been placed in the group of the brown algae, particularly in the neighbourhood of the Laminaria-like plants. These algae can attain a huge size (up to 70 m) and they grow often in submarine forests. In this case the plants develop a kind of trunk (called cauloid) with leaf-like structures on top (phylloids). The alga is attached to the sea bottom by root-like structures, called rhizoids.

In 1930 Kräusel and Weyland described leafy structures, attached to a stem of Prototaxites. Unfortunately they didn't picture them and furthermore these fossils disappeared in the war. Later on 'phylloids' have been found in Germany associated with Prototaxites, but not attached.

Jonker (1979) also described leaves attached to stems of Prototaxites, but in this case it has been demonstrated that they were not leaves but very thin layers of sediment. It has also been proposed that the enigmatic organism Nematothallus, which is a black patch of a couple of centimeters with a mat of thin threads or tubes underneath, could have been a kind of leaf-like structure of Prototaxites. But this plant has never been found attached to Prototaxites either. Summarizing it can be said that there is no convincing proof that leaf-like structures were attached to Prototaxites trunks.

Furthermore it is striking that the alga(?) Pachytheca is very often found in the same layers as Prototaxites (click on the photo). This fact has led to speculations that Pachytheca and Prototaxites perhaps originate from the same organism. But in this case no proof has been found either.

MOSELLOPHYTON

The most inportant defender of the alga theory at the moment is Dr. H.-J. Schweitzer from Bonn (Germ.). He has renamed a plant which was described in 1974 as Mosellophyton hefteri, in Prototaxites hefteri. This plant had whip-shaped branches and it lived in the tidal zones. Most of its fossils have been found in the quarries of Alken and Waxweiler in Germany. On the right is the restoration of this plant by Schweitzer.

It is remarkable that Schweitzer includes this plant in de genus Prototaxites because hardly ever more branched parts of Prototaxites are found. He is however relying on the transverse wrinkling of the surface of the fossil, which is also a property of the 'real' Prototaxites in the Eifel region.Unfortunately the fossils are only more or less compressed stems without preserved inner structure.

In 2000 he described the discovery of a branched stem of Prototaxites in the quarry of Waxweiler in the Eifel, which he interpreted as a part of the 'root' system of the alga Prototaxites. And indeed it resembles the rhizoid system of a Laminaria plant from the North Sea very much. In an attempt to solve the puzzle my wife and I went to Waxweiler and there we have collected in the Lower Devonian strata of the quarry.

The solution is probably that this plant is indeed an alga. Dr. Wutke of the new museum in Waxweiler on the conquest of the land (which will be opened in July), told me that he intends to call the plant "Mosellophyton" hefteri.

Schweitzer has always supposed that Prototaxites lived in the sea, but it has become clear now that it was a land dweller. In most cases the fossils are found in river or delta sediments. Mostly the trunks have fallen into pieces during the transportation in the river. The Taunus and Emsquartzite, which also contain (real) specimens of Prototaxites, is a sandy deposition near the coast. The Prototaxites are found there concentrated in some places, absent in other places. Schweitzer concludes that Prototaxites was growing in submarine forests along the coast, but it is also conceivable that rivers flowed into the sea in those areas.

Hueber shows in his paper that the structure of the cells of Laminaria-like plants in transverse section is quite different from that of Prototaxites. In the alga the cells are neatly ordered in radial rows and there is a clear division in pith, cortex and epidermis, but the hyphae in Prototaxites are dispersed randomly over the complete section.

The possibility that Prototaxites was an alga, can thus be put aside with an easy mind.

In 2002 Marc-André Selosse from Paris published a reaction on Hueber's paper on Prototaxites. He did value Hueber's research very much, but he had also serious doubts about his conclusions. Particularly on the following three points:

1. The remains of the reproductive structures, described by Hueber, are incomplete and not convincing. Furthermore it is peculiar that no spores have been found, not even in the direct vicinity of embedded specimens of Prototaxites.
2. The huge size of the fruiting body of the fungus cannot be clearly explained. Organisms become big in the competition with other organisms, but plants in the Early Devonian didn't grow much higher than 50 cm. Besides it is doubtful how the giant fungus could gain enough food. A rule of thumb is that the biomass in forests at a certain level of the food chain is at most about 10% of the next lower level. The fungi have a mass of about 10 % of the layer of humus in which they live. Prototaxites however seems to have had about the same mass as the layer on which it lived.
3. Prototaxites became extinct in the Late Devonian. Hueber thinks that this was possibly caused by predation by animals and by competition of trees and bushes. The latter however doesn't make sense, for fungi and plants are not food competitors and a fungus is not dependent on light. Plants only bring more food for the fungi.

Selosse thinks it possible to overcome these objections by assuming that Prototaxites was a lichen. That is a cohabitation of a fungus and an alga with mutual benefit (symbiosis). Fungi can gain minerals and water from the soil with their mycelium, whereas algae can produce nutrients from carbon dioxide and water by assimilation. Furthermore the alga and the fungus can give each other protection in very difficult circumstances.

According to Selosse the alga must have been situated near the outside of the youngest growth increment, because there light could be caught. The alga in the older (inside) parts died for lack of light, but the tubes stayed intact and because of their firm structure they gave stiffness to the trunk. The so-called skeletal hypha must have been the tube of the alga in Selosse's view.

Now-a-days algae which form tubes without septa do exist. In them growth is concentrated in the top and to prevent the flowing back of the protoplasm a temporary septum is formed. The rest of the tube is empty. It is possible that the alga belonged to this type. Moreover, green algae can produce chemicals which strengthen the walls.

The big size of the organism could have been an advantage because of the larger surface for the food production by the alga. Selosse mentions also the competition with plants but this argument certainly does not make sense for the Early Devonian.

An interesting and attractive ide is the possibility that the big size points at succulence. Cactuses can grow very tall and thick to collect as much water as possible in the scarce moments of rainfall. The absence of reproductive structures can be explained by assuming that Prototaxites used a vegetative form of reproduction. This occurs also in living lichens, e.g. when detached pieces develop to new individuals. In this case the extinction could have been the consequence of the competition as a consequence of densification of the vegetation.

CONCLUSION

All in all it can be concluded that the enigma has not yet been solved. Prototaxites will not be an alga, but perhaps it is a giant fungus and, who knows, the truth lies midway and it is a combination of a fungus and an alga, namely a giant lichen. At this moment the fungus theory is on the winning hand thanks to Boyce at al (2007). The idea of these giants is a bit uneasy, but we have now also accepted that dragonflies with a wingspread of 70 cm and dinosaurs sized up to 35 m have existed. And a time span of 400 million years is no negligible factor. Moreover, Jules Verne has already predicted in the Voyage to the center of the Earth that giant mushrooms could grow.

5

Wood of the Horsetail Tree Calamites

INTRODUCTION

Calamites is one of the most well-known fossils of the Carboniferous and the Permian. It is found as a stem with a longitudinal ribbing and, at some distance from each other, transverse lines or nodes. In most cases the stem of Calamites is flattened, but sometimes it is more or less threedimensional. In this case the fossil shows no internal structure: it is just petrified sediment. This is the reason that it is difficult to get an impression of the composition of the Calamites tree.

Rarely however stems and branches are preserved extraordinary well, i.e. when they have been mineralized as a consequence of exceptional circumstances. This is for example the case in the Lower Permian depositions of Chemnitz (Germany), where the trunks are silicified as a result of an enormous vulcano eruption. In the renewed Museum für Naturkunde in this city the worlds biggest Calamites trunk is displayed. And it is structurally preserved!

COAL BALLS

An other example of exceptional preservation is that of the coal balls. These are concretions of calcium carbonate and/or other minerals, occurring in some of the coal seams of the Upper

Carboniferous (Pennsylvanian). They have been found in the coalfields of Lancashire and Yorkshire in England and in several places in the USA.

Casts

The transverse sections of the two small trunks below show a serrated edge. In the stem on the left is an empty space to the inner side of the edge, in one on the right this space is filled with amorphous sediment. In young plants this central cavity was filled with thinwalled parenchym cells (pith), whereas in older trunks pith only occured in the outer regions of the central cavity. Most of the fossils of Calamites are casts of the central cylinder of the trunk. After the tree had died, this cavity got full of sediment, after which the bark and the wood of the trunk decayed. So only a cast of the central cylinder remained. The longitudinal ribbing on it is the counterpart of the serrate pattern on the inside of the central cavity. The transverse lines at the cast indicate where the diaphragms were placed in the central cylinder. These diaphragms or nodes are characteristic for horsetails. They gave rise to the wirls of leaves and branches.

In the transverse section the circle with the small round holes attracks attention. At the place of those holes the very first wood vessels (the protoxylem) of the young plant were located. These were of a very small diameter. Around them the metaxylem developed, also with very narrow cells. Next the secundary growth started from the cambium, a one-cell-thick layer of tissue, forming secondary wood to the inner side and no phloem to the outer side. It was a unifacial cambium. In the course of this process canals arose at the place of the protoxylem and the metaxylem. These are called carinal canals. So the holes are transverse sections of these carinal canals.

Between the successsive xylem bundles protrusions of the pith were formed: the rays. These are, however, not always present. In the latter case the secondary wood forms a unbroken cylinder. In the, rarely preserved, bark are air ducts at regular distances from each other. They are called vallecular canals. Because of these canals the outside of the living Calamites tree showed longitudinal grooves and ribs. This ribbing is seldom visible because the bark is hardly ever preserved. (Fig. 5.1)

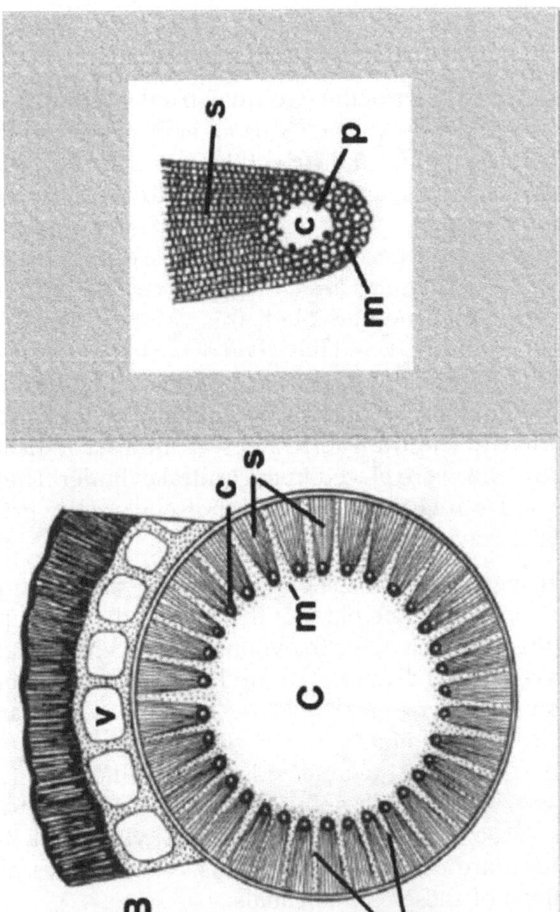

Transverse section of a stem of *Calamite*
B = bark, C = central cavity/cylinder, m = pith,
ms = rays, s = secundary wood/xylem,
c = carinal canal, v = vallecular canal

Bundle of wood vessels
c = carinal canal, p = protoxylem,
m = metaxylem, s = secundary wood/xylem
After Stewart & Rothwell, 1993

Fig. 5.1: Structure of a Calamites Stem

Genera

Three genera are distinguished in structurally preserved stems of Calamites. The above described kind of wood is called Arthropitys. It is the most common type. Moreover Arthroxylon and Calamodendron have been described. The differences are found mainly in the way the parenchym cells are situated amongs the wood cells. It is not certain whether these characteristics have systematical significance or not. It is possible that they have to do with development stages or with the place in the trunk.

Bordered Pits

To the left in the picture lay the pith cells, to the right the wood cells. The latter provide stiffness and they manage the water transport. They are called tracheids. The water moves from one tracheid to an adjacent one through holes in the radial cell walls. These holes are sometimes the centre of a so-called bordered pit, but ladder-like structures occur also.

Summarizing it can be said that the horsetail trees have achieved a maximum of solidity, thanks to a very efficient way of wood production. The cylindrical structure with a large central cavity appeared to work very well. The proof is that horsetail trees could reach a size of about 20 m. Their extinction will not have been caused by the woodstructure.

THE STEPHANIAN FLORA OF GRAISSESSAC

Graissessac is a former miners village in the Languedoc (south of France), not far from Bédarieux. In the course of years many fossils from the Upper Carboniferous have been found there, but the mining has been stopped years ago. At the waste heaps some fossils can still be collected.

The coal excavation in Graissessac was done in opencast coal pits. This means that first the overlaying layers were removed. This material was deposited on slopes at other places. Then the coal was extracted.

When we went collecting there for the first time, we could simply look on the slopes along the roads. Nowadays these slopes are almost completely overgrown and it is not possible to find there fossils anymore, except perhaps with great effort. Still there are some possibilities at places where waste heaps are being digged away.

About the Geology

The coal has come into existence in a so-called intramontane basin. During the Westfalian (the last but one level of the Carboniferous) the Hercynian process of mountain building (orogeny) was at his maximum. In the Stephanian the process came to an end and as a consequence of the 'relaxation' of the earth's crust small depressions, bordered by faults, came into existence, e.g. around and in the Massif Central. Graissessac is situated in such a depression. The new mountains suffered of a severe erosion and pieces of rock, sand and mud were transported downwards by mountain streams and rivers. In the valleys large swamps with abundant growth of plants came into existence. The peat layers are converted into coal seams in the course of 300 million of years and above these coal layers sediments with plant fossils are formed.

There are more intramontane basins in the south of France, e.g. near Alès (where the winning is still going on and where fossils can be found), Decazeville, Carmaux and Montceau-les-Mines. The latter sites have only poor possibilities now-a-days.

In Graissessac the coal has already been extracted since the 18th century and in 1918 the productivity reached its top. Around the year 2000 the last quarry has been shut down.

THE FLORA

The depositions of Graissessac certainly can said to be rich in fossils. Especially the group of Pecopteris, real ferns, is dominant in the flora, as can be seen in the histogram on the right. Many of the fernlike fossils originate from seed ferns, gymnosperm plants. But in Graissessac (and in the Stephanian in general) the real ferns form an important part of the flora. The total number of species we have found, is about 40 and this is an average result compared with other finding places. Many species of these 40 however are rather rare and some of them we have found only once.

Conclusion

Still it is possible to get a good impression of a number of important plants of the Stephanian: *Pecopteris, Odontopteris,*

Dicksonites, Pecopteridium, Sigillaria brardii and *Sphenophyllum oblongifolium*, to mention some of them. The club moss trees are strongly declining, the tree fern Psaronius with its Pecopteris-leaves is in a flowering time, the seed ferns Neuropteris and Alethopteris are getting less numerous, but they are replaced by other seed ferns like Odontopteris.

THE TREE FERN PSARONIUS

Psaronius is an extinct tree fern that lived during the Late Carboniferous and the Permian. It was most widespread during the youngest Carboniferous (Stephanian) and the Early Permian (Rotliegend). It could grow up to 10 or 15 metres high and wore a crown of Pecopteris leaves. The large number of Pecopteris fossils found in the Stephanian and the Lower Permian are an indication of the frequent occurrence of Psaronius. *Gymnospermous* and *angiospermous* trees have secondary growth by which they can form strong woody trunks. Tree ferns, Psaronius included, don't have secondary growth. They have developed another way to form a stable (false) trunk. The tiny vascular strand of the young plant while growing upwards divides into several parts, causing an upward broadening of the wooden kernel. At the same time a large number of adventitious roots are given off, forming together a root mantle. This root mantle gives the trunk its required stability. The base of the trunk of the tree fern is often thickenend because of the broad root mantle.

From the central strand of Psaronius also leaf bases split off. These were relatively thick because the leaves attained a length of 2 to 3 metres. The upper part of the stem didn't have a root mantle (yet) and below the leafy crown the scars of fallen-off leaves were visible. In lower parts of the stem these leaf scars were hidden by the root mantle.

In the region of the city of Chemnitz (Sachsen, Germany) many silicified trunks of Psaronius (and other tree species) are found as a consequence of a gigantic volcanic eruption in the Early Permian, about 290 million years ago. Especially the silicified root mantles yield, after sawing and polishing, beautiful images because of the fact that the woody kernel of the rootlets is star-shaped. That's why these fossils are called Staarsteine, meaning star stones. The cellular structure outside the wood kernels has not been preserved in most cases and the room has been filled up with agate.

Madensteine

Research on coal balls from the US has revealed that the leaves of Psaronius are of the Pecopteris-type. Petioles with attached fronds have been found. Many of the leaflets still bear the sporangia. These are fused in a characteristic way to synangia. Pecopteris-leaves with such synangia are called Scolecopteris.

At a couple of places in Sachsen, near Dresden and near Chemnitz, pieces of silicified rock are found containing Pecopteris/Scolecopteris leaflets. They are called 'Madensteine' because people thought them to be full of fossil maggots (Maden). The material of these Madensteine is called Hornstein or chert.

Tiny club-shaped objects with well preserved tissue have been found together with Scolecopteris /Psaronius. They resemble the mm-size first leaves of some extant fern and thus have been assumed to be very young plants of Psaronius emerging from a gametophyte. Early species of Psaronius are known from the Namurian of Scotland and the Lower Pennsylvanian of Illinois. In the Westfalian A and B this genus was still relatively rare but in the Westfalian C and D it became more widespread. In the Stephanian and the Early Permian Psaronius was most widely spread.

The various species lived in very diverse environments: wet lowlands, peat forming wet woodland, but also on periodically dry grounds. Psaronius disappeared only later in the Permian, when the climate became very dry and hot in many places. Another interesting fact is that in and on the root mantle many epiphytic ferns were growing. Also liana-like ferns and seedferns were climbing up along the Psaronius trunks. Stems have been found with up to eight climbing axes of one plant. Often the rootlets of these epiphytes are found among the rootlets of Psaronius. They are strikingly different in structure from the Psaronius roots.

6

Fossil Palm Wood or Palmoxylon

INTRODUCTION

In some regions of the Netherlands a lot of petrified wood has been found which is called palm wood or Palmoxylon. These are boulders probably transported by rivers and/or ice from Germany. In several states in the Unites States so much petrified palm wood is found that is has got a place of honour: it has become a State Fossil. This fossil is not always really originating from palms, but in most cases it is. The palms appeared for the first time in the Senonian (Late Cretaceous) and underwent their most important radiation probably in the Paleogene.

CHARACTERISTICS

Palm wood is characterized by the presence of a great nummer of thin tubes, laying dispersed on a transverse section of the wood. On the sides of the wood the tubes are running roughly parallel to the axis of the trunk. In the side view there are also little holes visible, because the tubes are rather flexuous. The diameter of all tubes is about the same. When there are thin as well as thick tubes, you don´t have palm wood but e.g. Tempskya.

Mostly the tubes are empty, but sometimes they are filled up. Looking through a loupe one will see that the tubes are not circular but that they have the shape of a moon during an eclipse. A transverse section of such a piece of palm wood makes this still clearer. Microscopic slides from material from the Netherlands show in nearly all cases a bad conservation of the internal structure. There are, however, exceptions in which the structure has been preserved very well in some places. The large white spot has been filled up with sclerenchyma cells, i.e. thickwalled cells providing stiffness. The three small white spots are transverse sections of wood vessels. The wood vessels are reinforced with annular and spiral thickenings.

THE STRUCTURE OF THE VASCULAR BUNDLE

One of the finest slides is the one which was bought in England by the Groningen University in 1922. It has been manufactured from a piece of palm wood probably originating from France. Besides the described vascular bundles there are also bundles which only exist of sclerenchyma cells. The diameter of these sclerenchyma bundles is very small compared to that of the vascular bundles. Their function is to give more stiffness to the trunk. Some of the vascular bundles bend off in a horizontal direction. These bundles are heading for a leaf and are sometimes called crossing bundles because they cross the other ones.

The Bark

Only in rare cases the bark has been preserved in fossil palm wood. Clearly visible is the fact that the vascular bundels are oriented in a certain direction: they are lying with the sclerenchymatic cap in the direction of the bark. Generally the orientation disappears as the distance to the bark increases. In the collection of Huis Bergh at 's Heerenbergh (NL) are a couple of specimens with preserved bark.

Wood or Not?

In fact Palmoxylon does not conform to the definition of wood. Wood in the narrow sense is secondary xylem, i.e. wood tissue formed by a cambium. All deciduous trees (dicotyledons) do have such a cell layer, which produces bark to the outside and wood to the inside. By far most of the monocotyledons, under which the palms, do not possess a cambium.

From the seed comes a young plant with rosette leaves, which is growing in the horizontal plane during a long period (1 to 5 years). In this way a firm base is formed from which later on the trunk can develop. After this phase several growth zones develop causing both increase in thickness as well as in height. In this way a trunk comes into existence completely consisting of primary wood tissue. As a consequence the thickness of the stem will not decrease while growing higher, like the stems of dicotyledon trees do, but stay in principle equally thick, although the thickness can show variation as a consequence of better or worse circumstances.

Palm or Not?

There are more monocotyledonous trees with a trunk structure like the palms. Examples are Dracaena, Yucca and Pandanus. Specialists are able to distinguish the fossils of the different groups. It is generally assumed that most of the Palmoxylon specimens are originating from real palms.

PRESERVATION

Palmoxylon fossils from the Unites States are often preserved much better than those in Holland. In Indonesia too palm wood of very good quality is found.

Obviously the Dutch palm wood has been fossilized under much worse conditions. Probably there was less silica dissolved in the water and/or there was less abundant water. Therefore the process of silification was going much slower.

Two factors were playing a role in the process of silification. First the permeability of the cell walls for the siliceous water, secondly the speed of the decaying process of the cell walls. The thinwalled parenchyma cells (the ground tissue) were decomposing very quickly, but they were also drenched very soon. The extremely thickwalled sclerenchyma cells decayed very slowly, but were nearly impermeable to water. The wood vessels and tracheids were rather thinwalled and easily penetrated by water, and besides they were resistant to decay because of the strong annular and spiral thickenings.

So the empty tubes in the Dutch palm wood are a consequence of the fact that the thickwalled sclerenchyma cells had been decayed before the silica water had penetrated the cells.

Roots

Palm trees have a lot of roots underground. On the lower part of the trunk often aerial or adventitious roots are found. These are partly embedded in the bark. Sometimes silicified wood of palm roots is found. For identification you need a transverse section and an expert.

It is amazing how few papers have been written on the subject of Palmoxylon. The standard work is the 300 pages article "Fossile Palmenhölzer" by Stenzel from 1904 (!). It is in German. Some other publications in German and in Dutch, but that was all. An important reason is probably that there are many uncertainties and traps in trying to identify species of Palmoxylon. But it seems that here is a vast unexplored field waiting for ambitious people.

7

Trace Fossil

INTRODUCTION

Trace fossils, also called ichnofossil, are geological records of biological activity. Trace fossils may be impressions made on the substrate by an organism: for example, burrows, borings (bioerosion), footprints and feeding marks, and root cavities. The term in its broadest sense also includes the remains of other organic material produced by an organism — for example coprolites (fossilized droppings) or chemical markers — or sedimentological structures produced by biological means — for example, stromatolites. Trace fossils contrast with body fossils, which are the fossilised remains of parts of organisms' bodies, usually altered by later chemical activity or mineralisation. Sedimentary structures, for example those produced by empty shells rolling along the sea floor, are not produced through the behaviour of an organism and not considered trace fossils. The study of traces is called ichnology, which is divided into *paleoichnology*, or the study of trace fossils, and *neoichnology*, the study of modern traces. This science is challenging, as most traces reflect the behaviour—not the biological affinity—of their makers. As such, trace fossils are categorised into form genera, based upon their appearance and the implied behaviour of their makers.

OCCURRENCE

Traces are better known in their fossilised form than in modern sediments. his makes it difficult to interpret some fossils by comparing them with modern traces, even though they may be extant or even common. The main difficulties in accessing extant burrows stem from finding them in consolidated sediment, and being able to access those formed in deeper water. Trace fossils are best preserved in sandstones; the grain size and depositional facies both contributing to the better preservation. They may also be found in shales and limestones

CLASSIFICATION

Trace fossils are generally difficult or impossible to assign to a specific maker. Only in very rare occasions are the makers found in association with their tracks. Further, entirely different organisms may produce identical tracks. Therefore conventional taxonomy is not applicable, and a comprehensive form taxonomy has been erected. At the highest level of the classification, five bahavioural modes are recognised:

- Domichnia, dwelling structures reflecting the life position of the organism that created it.
- Fodinichnia, three-dimensional structures left by animals which eat their way through sediment, such as deposit feeders.
- Pascichnia, feeding traces left by grazers on the surface of a soft sediment or a mineral substrate.
- Cubichnia, resting traces, in the form of an impression left by an organism on a soft sediment.
- Repichnia, surface traces of creeping and crawling.

Fossils are further classified into form genera, a few of which are even subdivided to a "species" level. Classification is based on shape, form, and implied behavioural mode.

INFORMATION PROVIDED BY ICHNOFOSSILS

Because identical fossils can be created by a range of different organisms, trace fossils can only reliably inform us of two things: the consistency of the sediment at the time of its deposition, and the energy level of the depositional environment Attempts to deduce such traits as whether a deposit is marine or non-marine have been made, but shown to be unreliable.

Paleoecology

Trace fossils provide us with indirect evidence of life in the past, such as the footprints, tracks, burrows, borings, and feces left behind by animals, rather than the preserved remains of the body of the actual animal itself. Unlike most other fossils, which are produced only after the death of the organism concerned, trace fossils provide us with a record of the activity of an organism during its lifetime.

Trace fossils are formed by organisms performing the functions of their everyday life, such as walking, crawling, burrowing, boring, or feeding. Tetrapod footprints, worm trails and the burrows made by clams and arthropods are all trace fossils.

Perhaps the most spectacular trace fossils are the huge, three-toed footprints produced by dinosaurs and related archosaurs. These imprints give scientists clues as to how these animals lived. Although the skeletons of dinosaurs can be reconstructed, only their fossilized footprints can determine exactly how they stood and walked. Such tracks can tell much about the gait of the animal which made them, what its stride was, and whether or not the front limbs touched the ground.

However, most trace fossils are rather less conspicuous, such as the trails made by segmented worms or nematodes. Some of these worm castings are the only fossil record we have of these soft-bodied creatures.

Paleoenvironment

Eubrontes, a dinosaur footprint in the Lower Jurassic Moenave Formation at the St. George Dinosaur Discovery Site at Johnson Farm, southwestern Utah.Fossil footprints made by tetrapod vertebrates are difficult to identify to a particular species of animal, but they can provide us with valuable information such as the speed, weight, and behavior of the organism that made them. Such trace fossils are formed when amphibians, reptiles, mammals or birds walked across soft (probably wet) mud or sand which later hardened sufficiently to retain the impressions before the next layer of sediment was deposited. Some fossils can even provide details of how wet the sand was when they were being produced, and hence allow estimation of palæo-wind directions. Assemblages of trace fossils occur at certain water depths and can also reflect the salinity and turbidity of the water column.

Stratigraphic Correlation

Some trace fossils can be used as local index fossils, to date the rocks in which they are found, such as the burrow Arenicolites franconicus which occurs only in a 4 cm (1.6") layer of the Triassic Muschelkalk epoch, throughout wide areas in southern Germany. The base of the Cambrian period is defined by the first appearance of the trace fossil *Trichophycus pedum*. Trace fossils have a further utility as many appear before the organism thought to create them, extending their stratigraphic range.

Ichnofacies

Trace fossil assemblages are far from random; the range of fossils recorded in association is constrained by the environment in which the trace-making organisms dwelt. Palaeontologist Adolf Seilacher pioneered the concept of ichnofacies, whereby the state of a sedimentary system at its time of deposition could be implied by noting the fossils in association with one another

INHERENT BIAS

Most trace fossils are known from marine deposits. Essentially, there are two types of traces, either exogenic ones, which are made on the surface of the sediment (such as tracks) or endogenic ones, which are made within the layers of sediment (such as burrows). Surface trails on sediment in shallow marine environments stand less chance of fossilization because they are subjected to wave and current action. Conditions in quiet, deep-water environments tend to be more favorable for preserving fine trace structures. Most trace fossils are usually readily identified by reference to similar phenomena in modern environments. However, the structures made by organisms in recent sediment have only been studied in a limited range of environments, mostly in coastal areas, including tidal flats.

Evolution

The earliest complea trace fossils, not including microbial traces such as stromatolites, date to 2000 to 1800 million years ago. This is far too early for them to have an animal origin and they are thought to have been formed by amoedae. Putative "burrows" dating as far back as 1,100 million years may have been made by animals which fed on the undersides of microbial mats, which would have shielded them from a chemically unpleasant ocean however their uneven width and tapering ends make a biological origin difficult to defend. The first evidence of burrowing which is widely accepted dates to the Ediacaran period, around 570 million years ago. During this period, burrows are horizontal, or just below the surface. Such burrows must have been made by motile organisms with heads, which would probably have been bilateran animals. The burrows observed imply simple behaviour, and point to organisms feeding above the surface and burrowing for protection from predators. The complex, efficient feeding traces common from the start of the ensuing Cambrian period are absent. Some Ediacaran fossils, especially discs, have been interpreted tentatively as trace fossils, but this hypothesis has not gained widespread acceptance. As well as burrows, some trace fossils have been found directly associated with an Ediacaran fossil. *Yorgia* and *Dickinsonia* are often found at the end of long pathways of trace fossils matching their shape; the method of formation of these disconnected and overlapping fossils largely remains a mystery. The potential mollusc Kimberella is associated with scratch marks thought to have been formed by its radula, further traces from 555 million years ago appear to imply active crawling or burrowing activity.

As the Cambrian got underway, new forms of trace fossil appeared, including vertical burrows and traces normally attributed to arthropods. These represent a "widening of the behavioural repertoire", both in terms of abundance and complexity.

Trace fossils are a particularly significant source of data from this period because they represent a data source that is not directly connected to the presence of easily-fossilized hard parts, which are rare during the Cambrian. Whilst exact assignment of trace fossils to their makers is difficult, the trace fossil record seems to indicate that at the very least, large, bottom-dwelling, bilaterally symmetrical organisms were rapidly diversifying during the early Cambrian. Further, less rapid diversification occurred since, and many traces have been converged upon independently by unrelated groups of organisms.

Trace fossils also provide our earliest evidence of animal life on land. The earliest arthropod trackways date to the Cambro-Ordovician and trackways from the Ordovician Tumblagooda sandstone allow the behaviour of these organisms to be determined The enigmatic trace fossil Climactichnites may represent an earlier still terrestrial trace, perhaps made by a slug-like organism.

COMMON ICHNOGENERA

- *Skolithos:* One well-known occurrence of Cambrian trace fossils from this period is the famous 'Pipe Rock' of northwest Scotland. The 'pipes' that give the rock its name are closely packed straight tubes — which were presumably made by some kind of worm-like organism. The name given to this type of tube or burrow is *Skolithos*, which may be 30 cm (12") in length and between 2 to 4 cm (0.8 to 1.6") in diameter. Such traces are known worldwide from sands and sandstones deposited in shallow water environments, from the Cambrian period (542 to 488 m.y.a) onwards.
- *Chondrites* are small branching burrows of the same diameter, which superficially resemble the roots of a plant. The most likely candidate for having constructed these burrows is a nematode (roundworm). *Chondrites* are found in marine sediments from the Cambrian period of the Paleozoic onwards. They are especially common in sediments which were deposited in reduced-oxygen environments.

- *Rusophycus* are bilobed "resting traces" associated with trilobites and other arthropodes such horseshoe crabs.
- *Trypanites* are elongated cylindrical borings in calcareous substrates such as shells, carbonate hardgrounds and limestones.
- Cruziana are excavation trace marks made on the sea floor which have a two-lobed structure with a central groove. The lobes are covered with scratch marks made by the legs of the excavating organism, usually a trilobite or allied arthropod and, in fact, several different types of trilobite have been discovered at the end of Cruziana trails Cruziana are most common in marine sediments formed during the Paleozoic era, particularly in rocks from the Cambrian and Ordovician periods. Over 30 species of Cruziana have been identified.
- *Thalassinoides* are burrows which occur parallel to the bedding plane of the rock and are extremely abundant in rocks, worldwide, from the Jurassic period onwards. They are repeatedly branched, with a slight swelling present at the junctions of the tubes. The burrows are cylindrical and vary from 2 to 5 cm (0.8" to 2") in diameter. Thalassinoides sometimes contain scratch marks, droppings or the bodily remains of the crustaceans which made them.
- *Asteriacites* is the name given to the five-rayed fossils found in rocks and they record the resting place of starfish on the sea floor. Asteriacites are found in European and American rocks, from the Ordovician period onwards; and are numerous in rocks from the Jurassic period of Germany.
- *Rhizocorallium* is a type of burrow, the inclination of which is typically within 10° of the bedding planes of the sediment. These burrows can be very large, over a meter long in sediments that show good preservation, e.g. Jurassic rocks of the Yorkshire Coast (eastern United Kingdom), but the width is usually only up to 2 cm, restricted by the size of the organisms producing it. It is thought that they represent fodinichnia as the animal (probably a nematode) scoured the sediment for food.

- *Teichichnus* has a distinctive form produced by the stacking of thin 'tongues' of sediment, atop one another. They are again believed to be fodinichnia, with the organism adopting the habit of retracing the same route through varying heights of the sediment, which would allow it to avoid going over the same area. These 'tongues' are often quite sinuous, reflecting perhaps a more nutrient-poor environment in which the feeding animals had to cover a greater area of sediment, in order to acquire sufficient nourishment.
- *Protichnites* consists of two rows of tracks and a linear depression between the two rows. The tracks are believed to have been made by the walking appendages of arthropods. The linear depression is thought to be the result of a dragging tail. The structures bearing this name were typically made on the tidal flats of Paleozoic seas, but similar ones extend into the Cenozoic.
- *Climactichnites* is the name given to trackways that usually consist of two parallel ridges separated by chevron-shaped raised cross bars. They somewhat resemble tire tracks, and are larger (typically about four inches wide) than most of the other trace fossils made by invertebrates. The tracks were produced on sandy tidal flats during late Cambrian time. While the identity of the animal is still conjectural, it may have been a large slug-like animal - its trackways produced as it crawled over and processed the wet sand to obtain food.

Other Notable Trace Fossils

Less ambiguous than the above ichnogenera, are the traces left behind by invertebrates such as *Hibbertopterus*, a giant "sea scorpion" or eurypterid of the early Paleozoic era. This marine arthropod produced a spectacular hibbertopteroid track preserved in Scotland.

Bioerosion through time has produced a magnificent record of borings, gnawings, scratchings and scrapings on hard substrates. These trace fossils are usually divided into macroborings and microborings. Bioerosion intensity and diversity is punctuated by two events. One is called the Ordovician Bioerosion Revolution and the other was in the Jurassic For a comprehensive bibliography of the bioerosion literature, please see the External links below.

The oldest types of tetrapod tail-and-foot prints date back to the latter Devonian period. These vertebrate impressions have been found in Ireland, Scotland, Pennsylvania, and Australia.

Important human trace fossils are the Laetoli (Tanzania) footprints, imprinted in volcanic ash 3.7 million years ago (mya) — probably by an early Australopithecus.

CONFUSION WITH OTHER TYPES OF FOSSILS

Trace fossils should not be confused with body casts. The Ediacara biota, for instance, primarily comprises the casts of organisms in sediment. Early geologists gave the name 'fucoid' to a wide variety of markings they found on the bedding planes of sedimentary rocks. The earth scientists frequently misinterpreted these 'fucoid' marks as being the fossilized remains of seaweed. However, in more recent years, these markings have been studied with greater thoroughness. It is now apparent that the 'fucoids' and other markings have in fact been caused by a variety of plants and animals. As a result, these 'fucoid' markings are now termed trace fossils.

Pseudofossils, which are not true fossils, should also not be confused with ichnofossils, which are true indications of prehistoric life.

TRACE FOSSIL CLASSIFICATION

Trace fossils are classified in various ways for different purposes. Traces can be classified taxonomically (by morphology), ethologically (by behaviour), and toponomically, that is, according to their relationship to the surrounding sedimentary layers. Outside of special cases, phylogenetic classification of trace fossils is unsatisfactory because the makers of most trace fossils are unknown.

Taxonomic Classification of Trace Fossils

The taxonomic classification of trace fossils parallels the taxonomic classification of organisms under the International

Code of Zoological Nomenclature. In trace fossil nomenclature a Latin binominal name is used, just as in animal and plant taxonomy, with a genus and specific epithet. When talking about trace fossils the genus is called an *ichnogenus*, and the species is an ichnospecies, the *ichno-* prefix coming from the Greek ikhnos, meaning "trace". The name is similarly italicized, and in full reference the author plus the year of publication should be cited. "Ichnogenus" and "ichnospecies" are commonly abbreviated as "igen." and "isp.", respectively.

Most researchers classify trace fossils only as far as the ichnogenus rank, based upon trace fossils that resemble each other in morphology but have subtle differences. Some authors have constructed detailed hierarchies up to ichnosuperclass, recognizing such fine detail as to identify ichnosuperorder and ichnoinfraclass, but such attempts are controversial.

The most promising cases of phylogenetic classification are those in which similar trace fossils show details complex enough to deduce the makers, such as bryozoan borings, large trilobite trace fossils such as Cruziana, and vertebrate footprints. However, most trace fossils lack sufficiently complex details to allow such classification.

Ethologic Classification of Trace Fossils

The Seilacherian System

Adolf Seilacher was the first to propose a broadly accepted ethological basis for trace fossil classification. He recognized that most trace fossils are created by animals in one of five main behavioural activities, and named them accordingly:

- *Cubichnia* are the traces of organisms left on the surface of a soft sediment. This behaviour may simply be resting as in the case of a starfish, but might also evidence the hiding place of prey, or even the ambush position of a predator.
- *Domichnia* are dwelling structures that reflect the life positions of organisms, for example the subsurface burrows or borings of suspension feeders, and are perhaps the most common of the established ethological classes.

- *Fodinichnia* are feeding traces which are formed as a result of organisms disturbing the sediment in their search for food. They are normally created by deposit feeders as they tunnel through soft sediments, usually producing a 3D structure.
- *Pascichnia* are a different type of feeding trace for which the trophic guild responsible are grazers. They create 2D features as they scour the surface of a hard or soft substrate in order to obtain nutriment.
- *Repichnia* are locomotory tracks that show evidence of organisms moving from one station to another, usually in a near-straight to slightly curved line. Most of the very few traces to be verifiably assigned to a specific organism are in this category, such as various arthropod and vertebrate trackways.

Other Ethological Classes

Since the inception of behavioural categorization, several other ethological classes have been suggested and accepted, as follows:

- *Aedificichnia* vidence of organisms building structures outside of the infaunal realm, such as termite mounds or wasp nests.
- *Agrichnia* so called "gardening traces", which are systematic burrow networks designed to capture migrating meiofauna or perhaps even to culture bacteria. The organism would have continually inspected this burrow system to prey on any smaller organisms that strayed into it.
- *Calichnia*: structures that were created by organisms specifically for breeding purposes, e.g. bee cells.
- *Equilibrichnia* burrows within the sediment that show evidence for organisms' responses to variations in sedimentation rate (i.e. the burrow moves upwards to avoid burial, or downwards to avoid exposure). Typically this evidence will be in the form of spreiten, which are small laminations in the sediment that reflect previous positions the organisms were in.

- *Fugichnia:* "escape traces" that are formed as a result of organisms' attempts to escape burial in sudden high-sedimentation events like turbidity currents. The burrows are often marked with chevron patterns showing the upward direction the organisms were tunnelling.
- *Praedichnia* trace fossils that show evidence of predatory behaviour, such as the drill holes (borings) left in shells by carnivorous gastropods, or more dramatically, the bite marks found on some vertebrate bones.

Over the years several other behavioural groups have been proposed, but in general they have been quickly discarded by the ichnological community. Some of the failed proposals are listed below, with a brief description.

- *Chemichnia:* a type of agrichnia applied specifically to those instances of bacterial harvesting.
- *Cecidoichnia:* a plant trace in which a gall is left on the plant as a result of interaction with animals, bacteria, or other plants.
- *Corrosichnia:* traces that are left by plant roots as a result of their corrosive action on the sediments.
- *Cursichnia:* a subgroup of the repichnia, created by a crawling or walking habit.
- *Fixichnia:* traces left by sessile organisms that anchored themselves to a hard substrate.
- *Mordichnia:* a praedichnial subgroup that shows evidence of the prey's death as a result of the attack.
- *Natichnia:* a type of repichnia caused by disturbances to a soft sediment by a swimming organism, e.g. a benthic fish.
- *Polychresichnia:* traces that show an origin in the combination of two or more established trace-producing behaviours, e.g. domichnia that served as the feeding position of the organisms.
- *Sphenoichnia:* a plant trace created by the bioturbational action of roots.

- *Taphichnia:* fugichnia in which the organism failed to escape and was buried, often resulting in its body fossil being found in association with the trace.
- *Volichnia:* traces that show the position a flying organism (usually an insect) landed on a soft sediment.

Fixichnia is perhaps the group with the most weight as a candidate for the next accepted ethological class, being not fully described by any of the eleven currently accepted categories. There is also potential for the three plant traces (cecidoichnia, corrosichnia and sphenoichnia) to gain recognition in coming years, with little attention having been paid to them since their proposal.

Toponomic Classification of Trace Fossils

Another way to classify trace fossils is to look at their relation to the sediment of origin. Martinsson s provided the most widely accepted of such systems, identifying four distinct classes for traces to be separated in this regard:

- *Endichnia* are those traces that are found wholly within the casting medium, and therefore can only have been made by an infaunal organism.
- *Epichnia* are found on the tops of the strata of origin, being those ridges and grooves that were formed by benthic organisms or infaunal burrows that have been exposed by erosion.
- *Exichnia* are traces that are made of material that is different from the surrounding medium, having either been actively filled by an organism or eroded out and re-covered by an alien sediment.
- *Hypichnia* are ridges and grooves found on the soles of the beds of origin at their interfaces with other strata, representing the opposite of epichnia.

8

Petrified Wood

INTRODUCTION

Petrified wood (from the Greek root "petro" meaning "rock" or "stone", literally "wood turned into stone") is a type of fossil: it consists of fossil wood where all the organic materials have been replaced with minerals (most often a silicate, such as quartz), while retaining the original structure of the wood. The petrifaction process occurs underground, when wood becomes buried under sediment and is initially preserved due to a lack of oxygen. Mineral-rich water flowing through the sediment deposits minerals in the plant's cells and as the plant's lignin and cellulose decay away, a stone mould forms in its place. It probably takes less than 100 years for wood to petrify.

Elements such as manganese, iron and copper in the water/mud during the petrification process give petrified wood a variety of color ranges. Pure quartz crystals are colorless, but when contaminants are added to the process the crystals take on a yellow, red or other tint.

Following is a list of contaminating elements and related colour hues:

- carbon - black
- cobalt - green/blue
- chromium - green/blue

- copper - green/blue
- iron oxides - red, brown, and yellow
- manganese - pink/orange
- manganese oxides - black/yellow

Petrified wood can preserve the original structure of the wood in all its detail, down to the microscopic level. Structures such as tree rings and the various tissues are often observed features. Petrified wood has a Mohs hardness of 7, the same as quartz. Petrified wood is the provincial stone of Alberta and also the state gem of Washington.

LOCATIONS

- Argentina - Considered to be one of the world's best petrified reserves, the Petrified Forest National Monument in Chubut Province in the Argentine Patagonia has many trees that measure more than 3 m (10 ft) in diameter and 30 m (100 ft) long. Compared to petrified trees in the United States that measure less than 1.8 m (6 ft) in diameter, the trees of the Central Steppes of Argentina are significantly larger.
- Belgium - Geosite Goudberg near Hoegaarden.
- Brazil - In geopark of paleorrota, there is a vast area with petrified trees.
- Canada - In the badlands of southern Alberta; petrified wood is the provincial stone of Alberta. Axel Heiberg Island in Nunavut has among the largest petrified forests in the world.
- Czech Republic, *Nová Paka* - The most famous locality on Permian-Carboniferous rocks in the Czech Republic.
- Germany - The museum of natural history in Chemnitz has a collection of petrified trees found in the town in 1737.
- Egypt petrified forest in Cairo - Suez road, declared a national protectorate by the minstery of environment, also in the area of New Cairo at the Extension of Nasr city, El Qattamiyya, near El Maadi distrect, Al Farafra oasis , Al Fayoum depression and actually the entire western desert.

- Greece - Petrified Forest of Lesvos, at the western tip of the island of Lesbos, is possibly the largest of the petrified forests, covering an area of over 150 km^2 and declared a National Monument in 1985. Large, upright trunks complete with root systems can be found, as well as trunks up to 22 m in length.
- Libya - Great Sand Sea - Hundreds of square miles of petrified trunks, branches and other debris mixed with Stone Age artifacts.
- United States - Some of the better known petrified wood sites include:
  - Petrified Wood Park in Lemmon, South Dakota.
  - Ginkgo/Wanapum State Park in Washington State.
  - Grotto of the Redemption, a private park in Iowa.
  - Petrified Forest National Park in Arizona.
  - Petrified Forest (California) in California.
- Australia - Has vast deposits of petrified and opalised wood.
- India - A geological site famous for its petrified woods Thiruvakkarai Village in Chennai, Tamil Nadu. The site is protected by the Geological Survey of India. Petrified woods covers a large area in this site.
- New Zealand - Curio Bay on the Catlins coast contains many petrified wood examples.

ARTIFICIAL PETRIFIED WOOD

Artificial petrified wood has been produced in a Washington lab. In the process small cubes of pine were soaked in an acid bath for two days then in a silica solution for another two. The product was then cooked at 1400 °C in an argon atmosphere for two hours. The result was silicon carbide ceramic which preserved the intricate cell structure of the wood. Soaking in a tungsten solution produced a tungsten carbide petrified wood.

COAL

Coal is a fossil fuel formed in ecosystems where plant remains were preserved by water and mud from oxidization and biodegradation, thus sequestering atmospheric carbon. Coal is a readily combustible black or brownish-black rock. It is a sedimentary rock, but the harder forms, such as anthracite coal, can be regarded as metamorphic rock because of later exposure to elevated temperature and pressure. It is composed primarily of carbon and hydrogen along with small quantities of other elements, notably sulfur. Coal is extracted from the ground by coal mining, either underground mining or open pit mining (surface mining).

Coal is the largest source of fuel for the generation of electricity world-wide, as well as the largest world-wide source of carbon dioxide emissions. Carbon dioxide is a greenhouse gas and these emissions contribute to climate change and global warming. In terms of carbon dioxide emissions, coal is slightly ahead of petroleum and about double that of natural gas.

Types of Coal

As geological processes apply pressure to dead biotic matter over time, under suitable conditions it is transformed successively into:

- Peat, considered to be a precursor of coal. It has industrial importance as a fuel in some countries, for example, Ireland and Finland.
- Lignite, also referred to as brown coal, is the lowest rank of coal and used almost exclusively as fuel for electric power generation. Jet is a compact form of lignite that is sometimes polished and has been used as an ornamental stone since the Iron Age.
- Sub-bituminous coal, whose properties range from those of lignite to those of bituminous coal and are used primarily as fuel for steam-electric power generation. Additionally, it is an important source of light aromatic hydrocarbons for the chemical synthesis industry.
- Bituminous coal, a dense mineral, black but sometimes dark brown, often with well-defined bands of bright and dull material, used primarily as fuel in steam-electric power generation, with substantial quantities also used for heat and power applications in manufacturing and to make coke.

- Anthracite, the highest rank; a harder, glossy, black coal used primarily for residential and commercial space heating. It may be divided further into metamorphically altered bituminous coal and petrified oil, as from the deposits in Pennsylvania.
- Graphite, technically the highest rank, but difficult to ignite and is not so commonly used as fuel: it is mostly used in pencils and, when powdered, as a lubricant.

Early Use

China was the only ancient civilization that possessed abundant coal resources. The earliest recognized use is from the Shenyang area 4000 BCE where Neolithic inhabitants had begun carving ornaments from black lignite. During the Han Dynasty coal was also used for fuel.

Outcrop coal was used in Britain during the Bronze Age (2000-3000 years BC), where it has been detected as forming part of the composition of funeral pyres In Roman Britain, with the exception of two modern fields, "the Romans were exploiting coals in all the major coalfields in England and Wales by the end of the second century AD" Evidence of trade in coal (dated to about AD 200) has been found at the inland port of Heronbridge, near Chester, and in the Fenlands of East Anglia, where coal from the Midlands was transported via the Car Dyke for use in drying grain. Coal cinders have been found in the hearths of villas and military forts, particularly in Northumberland, dated to around AD 400. In the west of England contemporary writers described the wonder of a permanent brazier of coal on the altar of Minerva at Aquae Sulis (modern day Bath) although in fact easily-accessible surface coal from what became the Somerset coalfield was in common use in quite lowly dwellings locally Evidence of coal's use for iron-working in the city during the Roman period has been found.

There is no evidence that the product was of great importance in Britain before the High Middle Ages, after about AD 1000. Mineral coal came to be referred to as "seacoal," probably because it came to many places in eastern England, including London, by sea. This is accepted as the more likely explanation for the name than that it was found on beaches, having fallen from the exposed coal seams above or washed out of underwater coal seam outcrops. These easily accessible sources had largely become exhausted (or could not meet the growing demand) by the 13th century, when underground mining from shafts or adits was developed. In London there is still a Seacoal Lane and a Newcastle Lane (from the coal-shipping city of Newcastle) where in the seventeenth century coal was unloaded at wharves along the River Fleet. An alternative name was "pitcoal," because it came from mines. It was, however, the development of the Industrial Revolution that led to the large-scale use of coal, as the steam engine took over from the water wheel.

Uses Today

Coal as Fuel

Coal is primarily used as a solid fuel to produce electricity and heat through combustion. World coal consumption is about 6.2 billion tons annually. China produced 2.38 billion tons in 2006 and India produced about 447.3 million tons in 2006. 68.7% of China's electricity comes from coal. The USA consumes about 1.053 billion tons of coal each year, using 90% of it for generation of electricity. The world in total produced 6.19 billion tons of coal in 2006.

When coal is used for electricity generation, it is usually pulverized and then burned in a furnace with a boiler. The furnace heat converts boiler water to steam, which is then used to spin turbines which turn generators and create electricity. The thermodynamic efficiency of this process has been improved over time. "Standard" steam turbines have topped out with some of the most advanced reaching about 35% thermodynamic efficiency for the entire process, which means 65% of the coal energy is waste heat released into the surrounding environment. Old coal power plants, especially "grandfathered" plants, are significantly less efficient and produce higher levels of waste heat. About 40% of the world's electricity comes from coal , and approximately 49% of the United States electricity comes from coal.

The emergence of the supercritical turbine concept envisions running a boiler at extremely high temperatures and pressures with projected efficiencies of 46%, with further theorized increases in temperature and pressure perhaps resulting in even higher efficiencies.

Other efficient ways to use coal are combined cycle power plants, combined heat and power cogeneration, and an MHD topping cycle.

Approximately 40% of the world electricity production uses coal. The total known deposits recoverable by current technologies, including highly polluting, low energy content types of coal (i.e., lignite, bituminous), might be sufficient for 300 years' use at current consumption levels, although maximal production could be reached within decades (see Table 8.1).

Table 8.1: Proved recoverable world coal reserves at the end-2006 [million tones (teragrams)]

Country	*Bituminous & anthracite*	*Sub Bituminous & lignite*	*Total*	*Share*
1	2	3	4	5
U.S.A.	111,338	135,305	246,643	27.1
Russia	49,088	107,922	157,010	17.3
China	62,200	52,300	114,500	12.6
India	90,085	2,360	92,445	10.2
Australia	38,600	39,900	78,500	8.6
South Africa	48,750	0	48,750	5.4
Ukraine	16,274	17,879	34,153	3.8
Kazakhstan	28,251	3,128	31,279	3.4
Poland	14,000	0	14,000	1.5
Brazil	0	10,113	10,113	1.1
Germany	183	6,556	6,739	0.7

(Contd...)

1	2	3	4	5
Colombia	6,230	381	6,611	0.7
Canada	3,471	3,107	6,578	0.7
Czech Republic	2,094	3,458	5,552	0.6
Indonesia	740	4,228	4,968	0.5
Turkey	278	3,908	4,186	0.5
Greece	0	3,900	3,900	0.4
Hungry	198	3,159	3,357	0.4
Pakistan	0	3,300	3,300	0.3
Bulgaria	4	2,183	2,187	0.2
Thailand	0	1,354	1,354	0.1
North Korea	300	300	600	0.1
New Zealand	33	538	571	0.1
Spain	200	330	530	0.1
Zimbabwe	502	0	502	0.1
Romania	22	472	494	0.1
Venezuela	479	0	479	0.1
Total	**478,771**	**430,293**	**909,064**	**100.0**

A more energy-efficient way of using coal for electricity production would be via solid-oxide fuel cells or molten-carbonate fuel cells (or any oxygen ion transport based fuel cells that do not discriminate between fuels, as long as they consume oxygen), which would be able to get 60%–85% combined efficiency (direct electricity + waste heat steam turbine). Currently these fuel cell technologies can only process gaseous fuels, and they are also sensitive to sulfur poisoning, issues which would first have to be worked out before large scale commercial success is possible with coal. As far as gaseous fuels go, one idea is pulverized coal in a gas carrier, such as nitrogen. Another option is coal gasification with water, which may lower fuel cell voltage by introducing oxygen to the fuel side of the electrolyte, but may also greatly simplify carbon sequestration. However, this technology has been criticised as being inefficient, slow, risky and costly, while doing nothing about total emissions from mining, processing and combustion.

Coking and use of Coke

Coke is a solid carbonaceous residue derived from low-ash, low-sulfur bituminous coal from which the volatile constituents are driven off by baking in an oven without oxygen at temperatures as high as 1,000 °C (1,832 °F) so that the fixed carbon and residual ash are fused together. Metallurgic coke is used as a fuel and as a reducing agent in smelting iron ore in a blast furnace. Coke from coal is grey, hard, and porous and has a heating value of 24.8 million Btu/ton (29.6 MJ/kg). Some cokemaking processes produce valuable by-products that include coal tar, ammonia, light oils, and "coal gas".

Peroleum coke is the solid residue obtained in oil refining, which resembles coke but contains too many impurities to be useful in metallurgical applications.

Gasification

Coal gasification can be used to produce syngas, a mixture of carbon monoxide (CO) and hydrogen (H2) gas. This syngas can then be converted into transportation fuels like gasoline and diesel through the Fischer-Tropsch process. Currently, this technology is being used by the Sasol chemical company of South Africa to make gasoline from coal and natural gas. Alternatively, the hydrogen obtained from gasification can be used for various purposes such as powering a hydrogen economy, making ammonia, or upgrading fossil fuels.

During gasification, the coal is mixed with oxygen and steam (water vapor) while also being heated and pressurized. During the reaction, oxygen and water molecules oxidize the coal into carbon monoxide (CO) while also releasing hydrogen (H2) gas. This process has been conducted in both underground coal mines and in coal refineries.

$$\text{(Coal)} + O_2 + H_2O \rightarrow H_2 + CO$$

If the refiner wants to produce gasoline, the syngas is collected at this state and routed into a Fischer-Tropsch reaction.

If hydrogen is the desired end-product, however, the syngas is fed into the water gas shift reaction where more hydrogen is liberated.

$$CO + H_2O \rightarrow CO_2 + H_2$$

High prices of oil and natural gas are leading to increased interest in "BTU Conversion" technologies such as gasification, methanation and liquefaction. The Synthetic Fuels Corporation was a U.S. government-funded corporation established in 1980 to create a market for alternatives to imported fossil fuels (such as coal gasification). The corporation was discontinued in 1985.

In the past, coal was converted to make coal gas, which was piped to customers to burn for illumination, heating, and cooking. At present, the safer natural gas is used instead.

Liquefaction - Coal-To-Liquids (CTL)

Coals can also be converted into liquid fuels like gasoline or diesel by several different processes. In the direct liquefaction processes, the coal is either hydrogenated or carbonized. Alternatively, coal can be converted into a gas first, and then into a liquid, by using the Fischer-Tropsch process.

The process of low temperature carbonization (LTC) can also convert coal into a liquid fuel. Coal is coked at temperatures between 450 and 700°C compared to 800 to 1000°C for metallurgical coke. These temperatures optimize the production of coal tars richer in lighter hydrocarbons than normal coal tar. The coal tar is then further processed into fuels. The Karrick process was developed by Lewis C. Karrick, an oil shale technologist at the U.S. Bureau of Mines in the 1920s.

In the Fischer-Tropsch process, an indirect route, coal is first gasified to make syngas (a balanced purified mixture of CO and H_2 gas). Next, Fischer-Tropsch catalysts are used to convert the syngas into light hydrocarbons (like ethane) which are further processed into gasoline and diesel. This method was used on a large technical scale in Germany between 1934 and 1945 and is currently being used by Sasol in South Africa. In addition to creating gasoline, syngas can also be converted into methanol, which can be used as a fuel, or into a fuel additive.

All of these liquid fuel production methods release carbon dioxide (CO_2) in the conversion process, far more than is released in the extraction and refinement of liquid fuel production from petroleum. If these methods were adopted to replace declining petroleum supplies, carbon dioxide emissions would be greatly increased on a global scale. For future liquefaction projects, Carbon dioxide sequestration is proposed to avoid releasing it into the atmosphere, though no pilot projects have confirmed the feasibility of this approach on a wide scale. As CO_2 is one of the process streams, sequestration is easier than from flue gases produced in combustion of coal with air, where CO_2 is diluted by nitrogen and other gases. Sequestration will, however, add to the cost.

The reaction of coal and water using high temperature heat from a nuclear reactor offers promise of liquid transport fuels that could prove carbon-neutral compared to petroleum use. The development of a reliable nuclear reactor that could provide 900 to 1000 °C process heat, such as the pebble bed reactor, would be necessary.

Refined Coal

Refined coal is the product of a coal upgrading technology that removes moisture and certain pollutants from lower-rank coals such as sub-bituminous and lignite (brown) coals It is one form of several pre-combustion treatments and processes for coal that alter coal's characteristics before it is burned. The goals of pre-combustion coal technologies are to increase efficiency and reduce emissions when the coal is burned. Depending on the situation, pre-combustion technology can be used in place of or as a supplement to post-combustion technologies to control emissions from coal-fueled boilers.

Coal as a Traded Commodity

The price of coal has gone up from around $30 per short ton in 2000 to around $150.00 per short ton as of September 26th, 2008. As of October 31, 2008, the price per short ton has declined to $111.50. In North America, a Central Appalachian coal futures contract is currently traded on the New York Mercantile Exchange (trading symbol QL). The trading unit is 1,550 short tons per contract, and is quoted in U.S. dollars and cents per ton. Since coal is the principal fuel for generating electricity in the United States, the futures contract provides coal producers and the electric power industry an important tool for hedging and risk management. In addition to the NYMEX contract, the Intercontinental Exchange (ICE) has European (Rotterdam) and South African (Richards Bay) coal futures available for trading. The trading unit for these contracts is 5,000 metric tons, and are also quoted in U.S. dollars and cents per ton.

Cultural Usage

Coal is the official state mineral of Kentucky and the official state rock of Utah. Both U.S. states have a historic link to coal mining. Some cultures uphold that children who misbehave will receive only a lump of coal from Santa Claus for Christmas in their stockings instead of presents. It is also customary and lucky in Scotland to give coal as a gift on New Year's Day. It happens as part of First-Footing and represents warmth for the year to come.

Environmental Effects

There are a number of adverse environmental effects of coal mining and burning, specially in power stations.

These effects include:

- Release of carbon dioxide, a greenhouse gas, which causes climate change and global warming according to the IPCC. Coal is the largest contributor to the human-made increase of CO_2 in the air.
- Generation of hundred of millions of tons of waste products, including fly ash, bottom ash, flue gas desulfurization sludge, that contain mercury, uranium, thorium, arsenic, and other heavy metals.
- Acid rain from high sulfur coal.
- Interference with groundwater and water table levels.
- Contamination of land and waterways and destruction of homes from fly ash spills such as Kingston Fossil Plant coal fly ash slurry spill.

- Impact of water use on flows of rivers and consequential impact on other land-uses.
- Dust nuisance.
- Subsidence above tunnel sometimes damaging infrastructure.
- Coal-fired power plants without effective fly ash capture are one of the largest sources of human-caused background radiation exposure.
- Coal-fired power plants shorten nearly 24,000 lives a year in the United States, including 2,800 from lung cancer.
- Coal-fired power plant releases emissions including mercury, selenium, and arsenic which are harmful to human health and the environment.

Economic Aspects

Coal liquefaction is one of the backstop technologies that could potentially limit escalation of oil prices and mitigate the effects of transportation energy shortage that some authors have suggested could occur under peak oil. This is contingent on liquefaction production capacity becoming large enough to satiate the very large and growing demand for petroleum. Estimates of the cost of producing liquid fuels from coal suggest that domestic U.S. production of fuel from coal becomes cost-competitive with oil priced at around 35 USD per barrel, (break-even cost). With oil prices climbing up to as high as 145 USD per barrel (posted on July 11, 2008), coal has become a viable financial alternative to oil for the time being, although current production is small.

Among commercially mature technologies, advantage for indirect coal liquefaction over direct coal liquefaction are reported by Williams and Larson (2003).

Intensive research and project developments have been implemented from 2001. The World CTL Award is granted to personalities having brought eminent contribution to the understanding and development of Coal liquefaction. The 2009 presentation ceremony will take place in Washington DC (USA) at the World CTL 2009 Conference (25-27 March, 2009).

The Energy Density of Coal

The energy density of coal can also be expressed in kilowatt-hours for some unit of mass, the units that electricity is most commonly sold in, to estimate how much coal is required to power electrical appliances. One kilowatt-hour is 3.6 MJ, so the energy density of coal is 6.67 kW·h/kg. The typical thermodynamic efficiency of coal power plants is about 30%, so of the 6.67 kW·h of energy per kilogram of coal, 30% of that—2.0 kW·h/kg—can successfully be turned into electricity; the rest is waste heat. So coal power plants obtain approximately 2.0 kW·h per kilogram of burned coal.

As an example, running one 100 watt computer for one year requires 876 kW·h (100 W × 24 h/day × 365 {days in a year} = 876000 W·h = 876 kW·h). Converting this power usage into physical coal consumption:

$$\frac{876\text{kW - h}}{2.0\,\text{kW - h/kg}} = 438 \text{ kg of coal} = 966 \text{ pounds of coal}$$

It takes 438 kg (966 lb) of coal to power a computer for one full year. One should also take into account transmission and distribution losses caused by resistance and heating in the power lines, which is in the order of 5–10%, depending on distance from the power station and other factors.

Relative Carbon Cost

Because coal is at least 50% carbon (by mass), then 1 kg of coal contains at least 0.5 kg of carbon, which is

$$\frac{0.5\text{ kg}}{12.\text{ kg/kmol}} = \frac{1}{24}\text{kmol}$$ where 1 mol is equal to NA (Avogadro Number) particles.

This combines with oxygen in the atmosphere during combustion, producing carbon dioxide, with an atomic weight of (12 + 16 × 2 = mass(CO2) = 44 kg/kmol), so 1/24 kmol of CO2 is produced from the 1/24 kmol present in every kilogram of coal, which once trapped in CO2 weighs approximately.

$$\frac{1}{24}\text{kmol}\cdot\frac{44\text{ kg}}{\text{kmol}}=\frac{11}{6}\text{kg}\approx 1.83\text{kg}.$$

This can be used to put a carbon-cost of energy on the use of coal power. Since the useful energy output of coal is about 30% of the 6.67 kW·h/kg(coal), we can say about 2 kW·h/kg(coal) of energy is produced. Since 1 kg coal roughly translates as 1.83 kg of CO_2, we can say that using electricity from coal produces CO_2 at a rate of about 0.915 kg/(kW·h), or about 0.254 kg/MJ.

This estimate compares favourably with the U.S. Energy Information Agency's 1999 report on CO_2 emissions for energy generation which quotes a specific emission rate of 950 g CO_2/(kW·h). By comparison, generation from oil in the U.S. was 890 g CO_2/(kW·h), while natural gas was 600 g CO_2/(kW·h). Estimates for specific emission from nuclear power, hydro, and wind energy vary, but are about 100 times lower.

Underground Fires

There are hundreds of coal fires burning around the world. Those burning underground can be difficult to locate and many cannot be extinguished. Fires can cause the ground above to subside, their combustion gases are dangerous to life, and breaking out to the surface can initiate surface wildfires. Coal seams can be set on fire by spontaneous combustion or contact with a mine fire or surface fire. A grass fire in a coal area can set dozens of coal seams on fire. Coal fires in China burn 109 million tons of coal a year, emitting 360 million metric tons of CO_2. This contradicts the ratio of 1:1.83 given earlier, but it amounts to 2-3% of the annual worldwide production of CO_2 from fossil fuels, or as much as emitted from all of the cars and light trucks in the United States In Centralia, Pennsylvania (a borough located in the Coal Region of the United States) an exposed vein of coal ignited in 1962 due to a trash fire in the borough landfill, located in an abandoned anthracite strip mine pit. Attempts to extinguish the fire were unsuccessful, and it continues to burn underground to this day. The Australian Burning Mountain was originally believed to be a volcano, but the smoke and ash comes from a coal fire which may have been burning for over 5,500 years.

At Kuh i Malik in Yagnob Valley, Tajikistan, coal deposits have been burning for thousands of years, creating vast underground labyrinths full of unique minerals, some of them very beautiful. Local people once used this method to mine ammoniac. This place has been well-known since the time of Herodotus, but European geographers misinterpreted the Ancient Greek descriptions as the evidence of active volcanism in Turkestan (up to the 19th century, when Russian army invaded the area).

The reddish siltstone rock that caps many ridges and buttes in the Powder River Basin (Wyoming), and in western North Dakota is called porcelanite, which also may resemble the coal burning waste "clinker" or volcanic "scoria". Clinker is rock that has been fused by the natural burning of coal. In the Powder River Basin approximately 27 to 54 billion tons of coal burned within the past three million years. Wild coal fires in the area were reported by the Lewis and Clark Expedition as well as explorers and settlers in the area.

Production Trends

World Coal Reserves

At the end of 2006 the recoverable coal reserves amounted around 800 or 900 gigatons. The United States Energy Information Administration gives world reserves as 998 billion short tons (equal to 905 gigatons), approximately half of it being hard coal. At the current production rate, this would last 164 years At the current global total energy consumption of 15 terawatt there is enough coal to provide the entire planet with all of its energy for 57 years.

The 998 billion tons of recoverable coal reserves estimated by the Energy Information Administration are equal to about 4,417 BBOE (billion barrels of oil equivalent). The amount of coal burned during 2001 was calculated as 2.337 GTOE (gigatonnes of oil equivalent), which is about 46 million barrels of oil equivalent per day. Were consumption to continue at that rate those reserves would last about 263 years. As a comparison, natural gas provided 51 million barrels (oil equivalent), and oil 76 million barrels, per day during 2001 (Table 8.1).

British Petroleum, in its annual report 2007, estimated at 2006 end, there were 909,064 million tons of proven coal reserves worldwide, or 147 years reserves-to-production ratio. It only includes reserves classified as "proven"; exploration drilling programs by mining companies, particularly in under-explored areas, are continually providing new reserves. In many cases, companies are aware of coal deposits that have not been sufficiently drilled to qualify as "proven". However, some nations haven't updated their information and assume reserves remain at the same levels even with withdrawals.

9

Plant Fossils

INTRODUCTION

Plants are often preserved as fossils. Leaves, which have fallen into the mud at the bottom of a lake, may leave behind carbon films and impressions that are preserved as the mud slowly turns into rock. A piece of wood, or even a whole tree may be quickly buried in sediment-the absence of oxygen stopping decay from occurring. Ground water then fills all the pores (or little spaces) in the wood with minerals, usually silica. The wood thereby becomes petrified, or turned to stone.

Coal is formed in a complex process from the partly decayed and compressed remains of ferns and other plants that grew in swampy conditions. Brown coal is generally of more recent origin than black coal and contains more water. Victoria's Latrobe Valley has large deposits of brown coal (less than 65 million years old), while black coal is found particularly in New South Wales and Queensland (200 to 300 million years old).

Plants have evolved over time. Australia's fossil record shows that during the Jurassic Period the dominant plants were cycads, gingkoes, conifers and ferns. In the next large time period, the Cretaceous Period, flowering plants made their first appearance. One of the oldest known flowers was discovered in 115-118 million year old rocks at Koonwarra (south Gippsland) in 1989.

Cycads

Cycads are sometimes called 'living fossils' because they reached their peak in the Jurassic Period (141 to 205 million years ago). Cycads are a member of the order Cycadales, which are the most primitive seed bearing plants. Like the related conifers (order Coniferales), cycads are cone bearing.

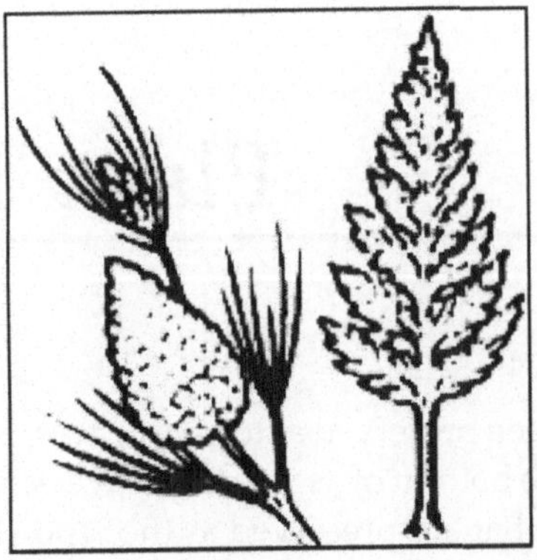

Araucarias

These ancient conifers reached their peak in the Mesozoic (251 to 65 million years ago). They are named after a group of South American Indians, the Araucani. The common names of the araucaria include the Hoop Pine, Bunya Bunya Pine, Norfolk Island Pine, Kauri Pine and the South American Monkey Puzzle Tree.

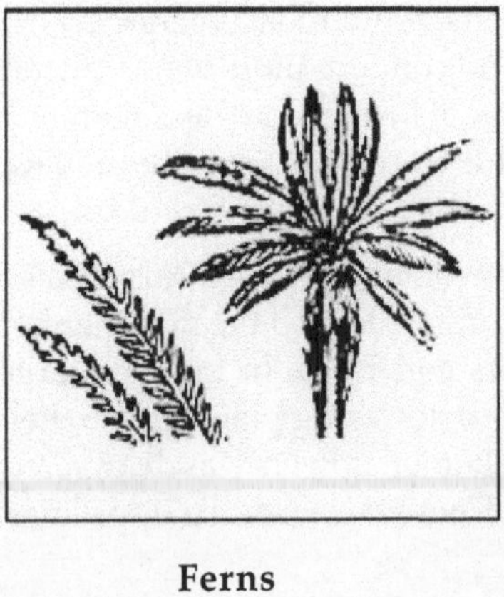

Ferns

Ferns are one of the most ancient plant groups surviving today. They first appear in the fossil record in the Carboniferous Period, over 300 million years ago. Ferns are now confined to fairly wet areas but once dominated the Earth's forests.

Gingkoes

Gingkoes have been found as 240 million year old fossils. The formerly extensive family of gingkoes has been reduced to just one species, Gingko biloba. The discovery of this species in the gardens of some Chinese monasteries a century ago surprised scientists, who had thought it extinct. Gingkoes are gymnosperms, and are therefore related to conifers.

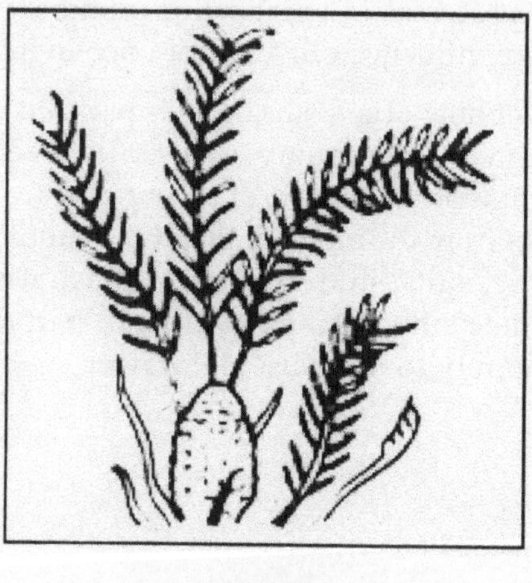

Cycads

PRESERVATION

The fate of most organic material produced by living systems is to be decomposed to carbon dioxide and water, and recycled into the biosphere. The circulation of elements through biogeochemical cycles indicates that decomposition is, indeed, efficient; however the presence of organic material in sedimentary rocks (e.g., coal, petroleum, dispersed organic matter, and fossils) shows that some organic matter - or its traces - escapes these cycles to be preserved in the rock record. The study of paleobotany relies on this preserved material - fossils - as evidence of past life. In the early history of modern paleontology, fossils were thought of mostly as static parts of the rock record ("sticks in mud"). This fostered description and classification as the main activities of scientific paleontologists. However, a shift in emphasis to thinking of fossils as "once-living organisms" gave paleontology a more biological flair and, more importantly, opened a new world of research questions. One tangible outcome of this philosophical shift is the movement of many academic paleontologists from Geology Departments to Biology Departments.

Plants become fossilized in a variety of ways. Each type of preservation carries different information about the once-living organism. Thus, an appreciation of plant fossils requires that one understand the processes of fossilization, and how each type of preservation may influence our view of once-living organisms.

The study of how organisms or their parts become fossils is called taphonomy. Taphonomy is literally everything that happens to an organism - or part of an organism, as is often the case with plants - from the moment that it dies until it is collected and curated for scientific study. Figure 9.1 illustrates some of the many taphonomic pathways a plant or plant part can take from it's living community to the museum drawer.

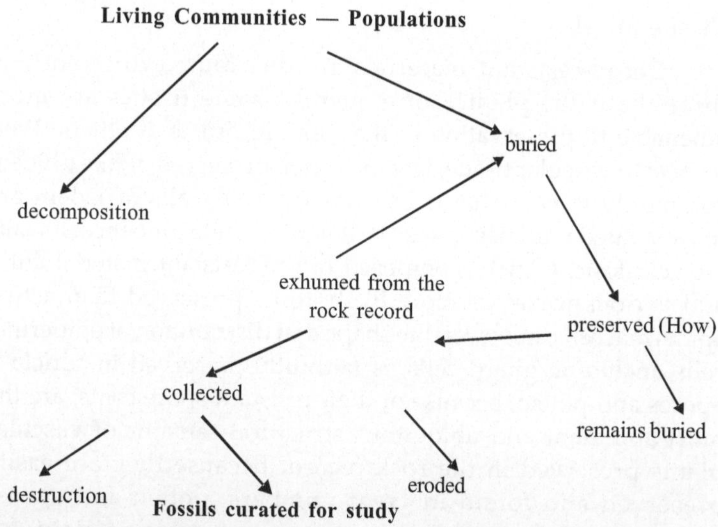

Fig. 9.1: Some of the many possible fates of plants or their parts as they enter the fossil record.

LEVELS OF PRESERVATION

Plant fossil preservation can take place at a number of levels. Each level contains a different type of information.

Cellular Level

Not all organic compounds are equally resistant to chemical degradation and decay. Plant cell walls (composed primarily of the polysaccharide polymer cellulose) are far more likely to escape decomposition than internal membranes and organelles, which are rich in protein, lipids and sugars. Preservation of cytological details has been reported in fossil plants, but occurrences are rare, and most reports of fossilized nuclei and organelles should be read with caution. Secondary compounds, such as those impregnating or covering cell walls, can also be resistant to decomposition; examples include lignin, waxes, cutin (which comprises plant cuticle), and sporopollenin, which forms the external shell of spores, pollen, and the resting cysts of some marine algae.

Tissue Level

Decay-resistant materials are distributed differentially throughout the plant. Consequently, some tissues are more amenable to preservation in the fossil record than others. With respect to vascular tissue, xylem is often preserved, while phloem commonly is not. This is because the cell walls of xylem are impregnated with decay-resistant lignin, while phloem cell walls are cellulosic. Cuticle, composed of the resistant material cutin and various waxes, is more likely to be preserved than actual epidermal cells; however, the shape and distribution of epidermal cells, including guard cells, is faithfully preserved in cuticle . Spores and pollen, because of their resistant spore coats, are the most abundant and ubiquitous structural remains of vascular plants preserved in the rock record. Because they are easily preserved and found in great numbers, pollen and spores (*palynomorphs*) provide important quantitative data for vegetation reconstruction and a variety of paleoecological questions.

Organ Level

Plants break apart, both in life (organ senescence or dispersal) and after death; dispersed parts may be transported before settling into the sediment to be buried and become fossils. Assemblages of plant fossils that are preserved close to where their parent-plants originally grew are called autochthonous; assemblages that have been transported are referred to as *allochthonous*. Whether an assemblage is *autochthonous* or transported has obvious implications for what sorts of ecological interpretations we can make from it. Therefore, as you study each type of plant fossil preservation, think about whether fossils produced in these ways are autochthonous or not.

The differential hydrodynamic properties of different plant organs often results in segregation of different parts in the fossil record. Some deposits contain only palynomorphs (e.g., pollen, spores, and a few other do-dads), while others may contain only large chunks of wood, or scattered leaves. Reproductive organs, especially flowers, are relatively rare in the fossil record because they are delicate and full of energy-rich, easily broken-down compounds. Other reproductive structures are sometimes preserved, however, and constitute a valuable source of taxonomic and evolutionary information. Fruits and seeds often contain resistant tissues (e.g., sclerenchyma) that yield clues to the reproductive morphology and biology of ancient plants.

The differential dispersal or plant organs before they enter the fossil record creates an interesting problem for the paleobotanist: We have to reassemble our plants before we can think of them as unified organisms. Botanists studying living plants take for granted that they know which leaves, wood, and reproductive structures belong to a species. For the paleobotanist, many of our plants come as isolated parts that have to be reunited. Obviously, the strongest evidence that organs belong together is actual organic connection. For example, we find leaves and reproductive structures both attached to a single branch. Another example is isolating spores from sporangia that are preserved on their parent leaf. Somewhat weaker inference is possible when two organs found in isolation have a unique, derived feature. For example, particular glands on the epidermis of stem, petiole, foliage and seeds allowed F.W. Oliver and D.H. Scott (1904) to unite these separate organs into a single form: the Devonian seed plant Lyginopteris. The weakest inference for uniting organs into a single plant species concept is when a suite of organs always occur together. However, a variety of other processes could generate this pattern and so caution is advised.

Because we don't always know which leaves belong to which seeds when they are first discovered, we use the convention of form taxa. When organs are found isolated (not in organic connection), each type of leaf and seed is given it's own binomial name (genus and species name according to the International Code of Botanical Nomenclature), without making any assumption about what belongs to what. To use the example discussed by Oliver and Scott (1904), leaves were described as Lyginopteris (genus only for brevity), seeds as Lagenostoma, and stems as Lyginodendron. The similarity of the first syllable gives a hint that the describing paleobotanists (others besides Oliver and Scott) suspected some relationship, but were unable to make a strong inference link. The last syllable of each name gives a hint to the organ type: "dendron" = stem, "pteris" is often used for frond-like foliage, "stoma" = seed. However, after Oliver and Scott's recognition of the unique glands on Lagenostoma lomaxi and species in the other organ form genera, they were able to make the whole-plant link with greater confidence. The whole plant then takes the name of the organ first described, in this caseLyginopteris. When you are writing, take care to make clear whether you are talking about form taxa (organs) or whole-plants.

Form taxa are not unique to paleobotany. For example, the planktonic larvae of many marine invertebrates are commonly described as separate species when they are first discovered in the ocean. Only later when they can be reared in the laboratory can the link to their adult form be recognized. Similarly, the different life stages of many fungi are given different names because they have different physical forms and hosts. Only through detailed inoculation studies can mycologists work out which forms are members of the same life cycle. Since some fungi may have more than five discrete life cycle stages, this can be a long process. Similar problems exist for some marine algae and multiple-host parasitic organisms of many kinds. Even among well-studied vertebrates, some tropical birds have been described as separate species until they are observed to mate and rear young together.

Organism Level

Not all plants in a given community are equally likely to find their way into the fossil record. Processes of fossilization often favor large or woody plants with resistant tissues over small herbs. Likewise, wind dispersed pollen is much more common in the fossil record than pollen dispersed by animals. Also, plants growing in or near an area of preservation (e.g., riverbank or swamp) are more commonly preserved than their counterparts growing far from water or anoxic sedimentary environments.

Environmental Level

Plant preservation depends on removing the organic material from the zone of aerobic decomposition. This is most easily accomplished by burying the plant. Consequently, swamps, deltas, lakes, lowland flood plains, and volcanic areas are good spots for fossilization. Arid regions and mountainsides are not likely candidates for plant fossil preservation (with the exception of exquisitely preserved plant material from Pleistocene packrat middens in the southwestern United States.

All of these taphonomic factors influence the information that can be recovered from the plant fossil record. While taphonomic filtering does not preclude biological interpretation of fossil material, taphonomy can introduce substantial biases into the record and influence our interpretation of the fossils, and thus our reconstruction of the ancient plants. It is, therefore, important always to keep in mind the mode of preservation of fossils when making any interpretations from fossils.

CONDITIONS REQUIRED FOR PLANT FOSSIL PRESERVATION

Three conditions are required for the preservation of plant fossils:

1. Removing the material from oxygen-rich environment of aerobic decay;
2. "Fixing" the organic material to retard anaerobic decay;
3. Introducing the fossil to the sedimentary rock record (a.k.a., burial).

Consequently, plant fossils are generally preserved in environments very low in oxygen (e.g., anaerobic sediment) because most decomposers (e.g., fungi, most decomposing bacteria and invertebrates) require oxygen for metabolism. Such sediments are commonly gray, green or black rather than red, a sedimentary signal of oxygen-rich conditions. The "fixing" requirements means that plant material must fall into an environment rich in humic acids or clay minerals, which can retard decay by blocking the chemical sites onto which decomposers fasten their degrading enzymes. Plant material can also be "fixed" by removing degradable organic compounds during the process of charring by wildfire. This is a common and spectacular mode of preservation for flowers. Plant material can then be incorporated into the rock record in areas where sediment is being deposited, which usually, but not always, requires the presence of water. Consequently, streams, flood plains, lakes, swamps, and the ocean are good candidates for fossil-forming systems. Plant fossils are commonly preserved in fine-grained sediment such as sand, silt, or clay, or in association with organic deposits such as peat (coal).

As you look at the various modes of preservation in lab, note the characteristics of the rock matrix in which plant material is preserved. Note color, grain size (i.e., sand, silt, clay), mineral composition (quartz, clay, mica, organic-rich, organic-poor), and any other unusual features. If you aren't familiar with the basic features of sedimentary rocks, they may start out all looking the sameÉdon't worry. Take some extra time to make systematic observations of each specimen: What color is it? Can you see the sediment grains with your naked eye? With a hand lens? How would you classify them (round or angular)? Is the rock shiny or dull? Does it have uniform or mixed composition? Do you notice sedimentary layers or other features (ripple marks, animal tracks)? Just be patient; you'll train your eye to recognize rock types in no time.

Types of Plant Fossils

Six broad categories of plant fossils are commonly recognized. Although these categories seem well-defined, a given fossil may fall into several categories or may elude them all. Consequently, these categories should be thought of as broad modes of preservation rather than shoe boxes into which all fossils must go. When thinking about types of fossils and modes of preservation, it is more important to consider what types of biologically interesting information is or is not present than to fret over strict classifications. With that caveat, the basic types of plant fossils include:

- *Compressions* — Two-dimensional, with organic material
- *Impressions* — imprints, two-dimensional, devoid of organic matter.
- *Casts and Molds* — Three-dimensional, may have a surface layer of organic material.

- *Permineralization* — Three-dimensional, tissue infiltrated by minerals allowing internal preservation.
- *Compactions* — Three-dimensional, reduced volume, flattened, wholly organic.
- *Molecular Fossils* — non-structural, preserves organic compounds.

Each type of plant fossil carries different types of anatomical and biological information. Consequently, to piece together the most complete picture of an ancient plant, paleobotanists hope for the same type of plant or plant part will be preserved in several different styles.

Compressions

Compressions are plant parts that have suffered physical deformation such that the three-dimensional plant part is compressed to more-or-less two-dimensions. Compressions retain organic matter, usually more or less coalified. Compressions of leaves, for example, differ from impressions in that some organic substance, often cuticle, is preserved. Peat, lignite, and coal are essentially compressions of thick accumulations of plant debris relatively free of encasing mineral sediment.

Compressions are excellent records of external form, especially for planar structures like leaves. They often preserve cuticle that can be recovered by dissolving the mineral matter in hydrofluoric acid (HF) or disaggregating in mild peroxide. The cuticle retains the imprint of epidermal cells, but other than this, cellular information can seldom be recovered from compressions. Consequently, compressions generally preserve plants at the organ, organism, and/or environment level. In addition, because compressions preserve organic material, carbon isotopic studies can be performed on compressions. From these studies, paleobotanists can sometimes recognize the biochemical signature of C3, C4, and CAM photosynthetic physiology in extinct species.

Study the assortment of compressions available. Note colour, texture, and type of deformation (usually flattening) experienced by each specimen. Notice distortion in original morphology is introduced by flattening.

Examine samples of coal, noting their weight, texture and surface features (dull vs. shiny). Identify discrete plant parts in the different ranks (essentially grades of metamorphism) of coal. Coal geologists recognize a continuum of degree of metamorphism in coal: peat - lignite - bituminous coal (A-C) - anthracite. Peat is an accumulation of virtually unaltered plant material, while anthracite is nearly pure carbon with little trace of the original plant material. All materials can be burned for fuel, but the energy content per weight increases with degree of metamorphism and the proportion of impurities generally decreases. Study thin sections of coal at the microscope. Can you identify specific plant parts in the thin sections? Study samples of fusain (fossil charcoal).

Impressions

Impressions are two-dimensional imprints of plants or their parts found, most commonly, in fine-grained sediment such as silt or clay. Impressions are essentially compressions sans organic material. If the sediment is very fine-grained, impressions may faithfully replicate remarkable details of original external form, regardless of sbsequent consolidation of the sediment. Study the specimens of impressions, noting the several categories of plant parts represened. Because of their shape, texture, and abundance, leaves are among the most common organ preserved in impression). Impressions may also occur if, when layers of rock are split apart, the organic material adheres to only one side of the rock. In this case, the side with organic material is the compression, known as the "part", while the corresponding impression known as the "counterpart".

One particularly interesting type of impression forms in "dirty" sand. In this type of sediment, relatively coarse sand grains are mixed with silt and clay. This type of sediment is comon in river and flood plain environments so is important for terrestrial plant preservation. When a leaf falls into this type of sediment and begins to decay, the first organic bonds to break leave charged molecular tails hanging off the leaf surface. This charged tail attracts clay particles with opposite charge that linger within the sediment. The clay migrates to the leaf surface, coating the organic structure. This has two remarkable consequences: First, further decay is retarded because clay is occupying sites of organic reaction. Second, the fine clay allows remarkable detail to be preserved. Because most of the sediment is relatively coarse (sand), the organic material is lost later, but an exquisitely detailed impression is retained in the clay film. This mode of preservation is important in the Dakota Sandstone flora of Cretaceous age. It is also important in the preservation of remarkable animal fossils such as the Jurassic bird Archaeopteryx and the strange Cambrian invertebrates of the Burgess Shale.

Impressions, like compressions, record information about external shape and morphology of plant organs. However, because they lack organic material, cuticle and organic carbon cannot be recovered from them. In cases of impressions in very fine-grained sediment, some cellular detail can be recovered by making a latex of silicone rubber cast of the impression.

Casts and Molds

When sediment is deposited into cavities left by the decay of plant parts, a cast results A mold is essentially a cavity left in the sediment by the decayed plant tissue. Molds are generally unfilled, or may be partially filled with sediment. Casts and molds commonly lack organic matter, but a resistant structure like periderm may be preserved as a compression on the outside of the cast or the inside of a mold. Casts and molds may be found together with the cast filling the mold.

Molds are formed when soft sediment surrounding the structure lithifies or hardens before the structure decays. When the mold fills in with sediment that subsequently hardens, a cast is formed. Casts of an internal hollow structure like a pith cavity are also common. Pith casts can be confusing because you are looking at the inside of the fossil-what in life would have been empty space. Like compressions and impressions, casts and molds record external (or sometimes internal) organ features well, but provide no cellular or tissue information. Unlike compressions/impressions, molds and casts often are truer records of the original three-dimensional shape of the structure. Casts of ancient trees are among the most impressive plant fossils

Permineralizations

Permineralization occurs when the plant tissues are infiltrated with mineral-rich fluid. Minerals (commonly silica, carbonate, phosphate or pyrite or rarely other minerals) precipitate in cell lumens and intercellular spaces, thus preserving internal structures of plant parts in three dimensions. This type of preservation is known as "structural preservation". Because organic material (commonly cell walls but in some cases finer detail) is preserved, permineralizations can yield detailed information about the internal structure of the once-living plant . When mineral matter actually replaces the cell-wall and other internal structures, the preservation may be called petrifaction. In petrified specimens, cellular details are lost with the organic material of the cell wall. Please note that we are using these words in a precise, scientific sense. "Petrified" also has a colloquial meaning that might encompass what we distinguish as "permineralized". Therefore, for the purpose of this course, permineralized wood preserves the cellular detail of wood anatomy and the lignin of cell walls that has been "fixed" by a mineral in-filling. This is much like bioplastic in-filling cellular structures when one makes a histological thin section. Petrified wood, on the other hand, lacks such cellular preservation.

Silica permineralization (silification commonly occurs in areas where silica-rich volcaniclastic sediments are weathering, for example the famous upright trees in Yellowstone National Park or nearby Calistoga, California. Silification is also an important preservational mode for Precambrian microbial remains deposited in near-shore marine environments.

Permineralization with calcium carbonate (calcite or dolomite) is particularly common in Carboniferous coal seams , where whole regions of peat were permineralized. Called coal balls (because of their sometimes round or ellipsoidal shape or widow makers (because of their tendency to drop out of mine roofs onto the heads of unsuspecting miners), these fossils commonly preserve a hodge-podge of plants and plant organs.

Permineralizations in pyrite (an iron-sulfur mineral) are particularly important in Devonian rocks where coal balls and well-preserved compactions are rare or unknown. These pyritized fossils often occur in the presence of sea water (a source of sulfur), and are characteristic of plant tissues washed into marine basins. Pyrite permineralizations offer a challenge to the museum curator because iron in pyrite exists in a reduced state and tends to oxidize when exposed to air. Upon oxidization, most of the structures are lost. This is called "pyrite disease" in fossils and is characterized by a mold-like appearance on the cut surface of the coal ball. To prevent destruction, the surface can be coated with a sealant. Coal balls can also be stored in an low-oxygen medium like glycerin or antifreeze.

Permineralization with phosphate is uncommon for land plants, but can be important in some types of marine settings.

Compactions

In peat, brown coals (lignite), middens and soft sediments, plant remains may retain their external form with only slight volume reduction due to compaction. Such tissues are not mineralized, retain resistant organic material, and may show unidirectional compression (flattening). Internal structure, especially of thick-walled, hard fruits is sometimes well preserved. These fossils may be sectioned by microtome or embedded and treated much like living tissues. Compactions are most common in the youngest plant fossils. Examine specimens of Tertiary fruits and seeds, and thin sections made from them. Pollen and spores are also preserved as compactions. The material making up their outer shells (*sporopollenin*) is extremely resistant to decay and can remain for hundreds of millions of year practically unaltered in the rock record. However, the pollen and spore shells, once spherical, are flattened by the compressive forces of lithification.

MOLECULAR FOSSILS

As more becomes known about the chemistry of modern plants, paleobotanists have begun to examine the fossil record for corresponding chemical data. For example, characteristic breakdown products of chlorophylls and lignins have been found in well-preserved fossil leaves. Lipids and their derivatives have also been recovered from sediments. Some carbohydrate break-down products may also survive in sediment. A special class of these, oleananes, are formed by flowering plants, some ferns and lichens. An increase in abundance of these molecules in sediments of mid to Late Cretaceous age is used to document the increasing abundance of flowering plants (Moldowan et al, 1994). In another stunning example, genetic material was recovered from Tertiary leaves, and the age of material from which DNA and RNA is recovered seems to be greater with every issue of Nature. As testament to the anoxic requirement for preservation of most molecular fossils, the RNA recovered from fossil leaves degrades within a few seconds when exposed to air, so special preparation techniques were developed to harvest and transport the material to the lab for processing.

Molecular fossils are recovered and studied using chromatographic techniques, mass spectrometry, and spectrophotometry. The preservation of these chemical products is highly variable, and depends on oxygen levels during deposition, temperatures experienced by the rocks since preservation, and many other physical and chemical factors. In a similar vein, geochemists have investigated the chemistry of petroleum and its precursors in an attempt to understand its formation.

Fossil DNA and RNA have also been making headlines in the scientific press. In some exceptional cases, genetic material or proteins have been sufficiently well-preserved to permit their use in the reconstruction of evolutionary relationships, in much the same way as one might sequence living organisms. However, much of this work is controversial due to the difficulty of preserving and isolating these fragile molecules. Also, contamination by other materials is a common and difficult to recognize problem.

A more mainstream application of organic chemistry to the study of ancient plants is that of stable carbon isotopes. During photosynthesis, plants reduce carbon from carbon dioxide to form organic molecules. This ratio of carbon 12 to carbon-13 in the resulting compounds gives information on the proportion of these isotopes in the atmosphere (interesting for geological questions relating to global carbon cycling) and about the physiology of the plant itself. In lecture we will discuss several applications of these techniques.

10

Plant Remains

INTRODUCTION

Soil samples for environmental analysis were taken from a representative selection of all ditch, pit and drain features. Seventeen samples were subjected to a system of flotation and wet-sieving in a Sirafstyle flotation tank. The floating debris was collected in a 250-ìm sieve and, once dry, scanned using a binocular microscope. Any material remaining in the flotation tank was wet-sieved through a 1mm mesh and air-dried. This was then sorted by eye and any material of archaeological significance removed.

SAMPLE ASSESSMENT

The archaeobotanical evidence was restricted to charred plant remains as ground conditions on the site were not suitable for preservation of organic remains by waterlogging. The majority of samples contained low concentrations of carbonized cereal grains, weed seeds and charcoal. In addition, a number of samples contained the carbonized remains of legume seeds.

The following report concentrates on the botanical element of the samples. Identifications were made with reference to the modern comparative collection of Headland Archaeology and seed atlases. Botanical nomenclature generally follows that of the *Flora Europaea*.

DISTRIBUTION

Carbonized plant remains were present in the majority of features excavated, albeit in low quantities. Plant assemblages were dominated by cereal grains, primarily wheat and barley. Some were in good condition but much was abraded. The highest concentration of cereal remains (over 300 identifiable grains) was recovered from context 019, the upper fill of medieval Pit 020.

Composition

Cereal and chaff remains Grains of wheat (*Triticum* sp) and hulled barley (Hordeum vulgare) were the most frequently encountered elements. Both bread/club wheat (T. aestivo-compactum) and spelt (*T. spelta*) were identified. One barley rachis internode was recovered from context 019. Grains of oat were also present in five of the samples. The lemma and palaea remained attached to one oat grain and this was identified as being black oat (*Avena strigosa*).

Wild Taxa

Small quantities of seeds and fruits of wild taxa were recovered from a number of the samples. The taxa present are typical ruderal/ segetal species of Northern Britain, ie species of agricultural fields and disturbed ground, including knotgrass (Polygonum sp), buttercup (*Ranunculus* sp) and dock (*Rumex* sp). High concentrations of seeds of vetch/tare (*Vicia/Lathyrus*), indicative of grasslands.

Other Economic Species

A number of charred horse/broad bean seeds (*Vicia faba*) were recovered from the two fills.

Roman Features

Low concentrations of carbonized plant remains were recovered from Ditches. The plant remains consisted of a mixture of cereal grain, weed seeds and an a remains included spelt, bread/club wheat, hulled barley and oat. Evidence from other Roman military and non-military sites across Britain indicate that these cereal species were being cultivated during the Roman period the plant assemblage from Cramond is therefore typical of this period.

Low quantities of abraded grain were recovered from context 038, the upper fill of the Antonine defensive Ditch 031. The presence of cereal remains within the upper fill could indicate that some domestic activity was being carried out whilst the ditch was still partially open.

The same deposit also contained a large number of carbonized and highly abraded seeds of *vetch/tare (Vicia/ Lathyrus)*. *Vetch/tare* seeds were the dominant plant remains recovered from the well, with over 120 identifiable seeds present. Both species are common elements of grasslands and arable fields.

Legume seeds are rarely recovered from Scottish Roman sites, the principal evidence for their use coming from samples taken from a waterlogged ditch fill at Bearsden. The waterlogged remains from that site included seeds of pulses, legumes and erbs, indicating that these food types were being transported across the Roman Empire. Documentary sources also indicate that beans and lentils were considered an important part of the Roman army diet. Written records indicate that horse/broad beans were either made into bean meal that was used in the making of bread, or cooked into a pottage that was fortified with pieces of meat or fish. There is little evidence, however, to indicate how the beans were prepared once harvested.

It is most likely that the carbonized horse beans present in the well fill at Cramond are the remnants of food charred either during food preparation or drying/roasting. Unlike grain, it is not necessary for beans to be dried prior to processing and they are therefore less likely to become charred. However, beans could have been dried in order to allow long-term storage or may have been roasted prior to consumption or milling. For instance, beans were recovered from a Roman drier at Odell villa, Bedfordshire, suggesting that the beans were being deliberately dried. The vetch/tare seeds recovered with the beans may be the remains of weed seeds that were contaminants of the bean crop.

Medieval Features

Carbonized plant remains were recovered from medieval Pits. The upper fill of Pit contained the largest single plant assemblage recovered from the whole site, with over 600 grains recovered. The most abundant element was cereal grain, with bread/club wheat, hulled barley and oat present. The quantity of grain is such that it seems likely that some sort of accidental burning occurred, either during corn-drying or through conflagration of a store, and the spoiled corn was dumped into the pit.

The mixture of cereals present is typical of Scottish medieval assemblages but the high percentage of bread/club wheat compared to oat and hulled barley is unusual. Hulled barley and oat were the more commonly cultivated cereals during this period in Scotland. The high proportion of bread/club wheat may be a reflection of the close proximity of the site to East Lothian and Fife where bread wheat was more readily cultivated and would in turn suggest a possible high status for the site.

Futures of Unknown Date

Carbonized plant remains were recovered from two features of unknown date, In both cases the amount of plant remains recovered was very sparse. The assemblage was predominantly cereal grain, with both wheat and barley present. This concentration of charred remains would be consistent with low-levels of re-worked material from the topsoil being incorporated into negative features and there is little evidence to suggest that the charred remains are related to the use of these features.

11

Plantation Establishment and Kyoto Protocol

INTRODUCTION

There are a variety of reasons why countries offer incentives for plantation establishment. However, it is difficult to design a subsidy programme that creates the intended effects without undue negative impacts. Subsidies have always been heavily scrutinized, since they inevitably disadvantage competing investments and distort the market. Scrutiny is intensifying as the processes of eliminating trade barriers and investment distortions continue apace.

Incentive programmes in Chile, India, and Indonesia will be described, including their structure, intended objectives, and actual impacts. The final section will synthesize the experiences of the countries sampled and develop conclusions.

Researchers defined incentives as "public subsidies given in various forms to the private sector to encourage socially desirable actions by private entities." Direct incentives include cost sharing, subsidized credit, fiscal incentives, reduction of uncertainty through loan guarantees, insurance, forest protection agreements, and provision of land tenure. Indirect incentives include provision of market information, extension and education, and research. The incentive programmes discussed here are provided by governments; projects funded by development banks and other foreign aid organizations are excluded.

Roles of Plantations and Reasons for Financial Assistance Packages

Why plantations? The traditional reason for plantation establishment is to provide fibre and other products such as latex, nuts, fruits, fuelwood, or fodder. Many plantation species provide multiple products during their lifespan. Plantations have been used to support forest industry expansion and this objective has often been twinned with the intention of reducing harvesting pressure on native forests.

Another traditional rationale for establishing plantations is to stabilize poor sites and reclaim sites depleted by logging, fire, or other agents. More recently, plantations are being viewed as precursors to the re-establishment of natural forests on degraded areas and as sinks for carbon dioxide. Utilities have been establishing plantations to offset their emissions and many countries are considering using plantations to help meet their Kyoto commitments. These ecological values can be very significant but are rarely considered by investors since they are difficult to quantify and compare with monetary values. Also, a private investor is unlikely to capture many of the social and ecological benefits from plantations.

Thus, a prime justification for offering incentives is to raise the private return to encourage a more socially desirable level of plantation investment. Incentives are appropriate when the private net returns are lower but the returns including externalities are greater than the returns from alternative land uses. In this situation, incentives could be effective by creating a more socially desirable land-use pattern. Incentives may not be needed if the private returns from forestry exceed those from other land uses or if the addition of incentives will still not provide an attractive private return. In selecting an appropriate level of assistance, rates of return not only have to be compared with those from alternate land uses but also with investments in other sectors.

Incentives may also be used to help investors overcome barriers such as the high capital cost of establishment and the relatively long waiting period for a return. Sometimes, investors, including local farmers, have a cultural bias against investing in plantations or they do not appreciate the advantages. Incentives may draw their attention to this sector.

In addition to these economic arguments for incentives, there may be strategic reasons. Countries such as Indonesia and Chile have used incentive programmes to jump-start the initial development of national forest industries, in part, to generate foreign exchange. Incentives may attract investment away from other countries, states/provinces or regions. However, the validity of this rationale depends on the competitive advantage of the forest sector with respect to forest production in other countries and relative to activities in other domestic sectors. There is also the risk of competitors retaliating by offering their own subsidies.

Incentives can be used to encourage economic development and generate employment in specific, less developed regions. If a large processing plant can be attracted to an area, it may act as a catalyst for infrastructure development as well as providing employment (often relatively highly paid) and attendant benefits. Incentives may also be a tool to diversify the economy in regions that are, for example, primarily agricultural, or to shift resources away from a sector with limited economic potential (again, agriculture is the most likely candidate).

Sometimes it has been claimed that forest incentives are self-financing in the sense that a substantial income may be generated over time and, if taxed, the government may at least partly recover its contribution. Chile's plantation subsidies are reported to have profited the state.

Macroeconomic and structural factors can have profound impacts on the attractiveness of plantation investments and the effectiveness of subsidies. For example, many African countries cited a shortage of capital as a major impediment to plantation investments. Other constraints include a lack of economic planning and project development expertise, unsupportive government policies, institutional limitations; inadequate infrastructure, the small size of domestic markets and currency devaluation. In addition, land-use policies and tenure rights are often weak and poorly designed.

Recent economic policy favours the direct elimination of distortions existing elsewhere in the economy rather than using subsidies as offsetting measures: (i) the removal of forest products export bans and tariff and non-tariff barriers to international trade of all products; (ii) the elimination of export subsidies; iii) the removal of all forest product consumption taxes other than the general sales tax. They argue that once these reforms are in place, direct incentives for forestry are unnecessary.

NATIONAL CASE STUDIES

Chile

In 1973, the Chilean government initiated a structural adjustment programme that reduced the role of government and provided leeway for the private sector to operate. Privatization was a key element of the reforms, which created a dynamic, export-led, market-based economy. The main elements included:

- (i) return of land and industries seized by the previous government to their original owners;
- (ii) privatization of public enterprises, banks, state-held lands, and the national pension fund;
- (iii) elimination of non-tariff barriers to trade and a reduction of import duties from an average rate of 105 percent in 1973 to 10 percent in 1979;
- (iv) a reduction in public spending and tax reform (resulting in a balanced budget in 1977);
- (v) elimination of interest rate and credit allocation controls; and
- (vi) introduction of a crawling peg and then a fixed exchange rate to help stabilize domestic prices.

Financial Incentive Programmes

As part of this reform package, a timber plantation subsidy programme was initiated in 1974 as part of Decreto Ley 701

(DL701), a forestry law. "The primary intent of DL701 was to persuade the private sector to assume the task of reforestation. The decree maintained some of the tax exemptions established in 1931 and added direct payments to the tax incentives. The key provision reimbursed 75 percent of the costs of reforestation." Further payments were available for additional silvicultural activities. The Chilean government also granted exemptions on property and inheritance taxes on reforested land and established a special Central Bank line of credit for reforestation. In 1975, the government began to sell its state-owned plantations, along with land, nurseries and machinery. This divestiture took four years to complete.

The incentive programme had an immediate impact, as private sector planting accelerated. The average annual reforestation level was 11,373 ha between 1940 through 1974 and there were about 300,000 ha of forest plantations in 1974, established largely by the state. In 1990, the plantation area had risen to 1.45 million ha, mostly established by the private sector. Plantation establishment rates averaged almost 80,000 ha annually from 1974 to 1990 and the proportion of reforestation performed by the state fell from a high of 91 percent in 1973 to almost zero in 1979.

The planting subsidy was removed in 1994. Since then, plantation area has continued to increase but at a slower pace. In 1995, Chile had an estimated 1,747,000 ha of plantations, with 96% or 1,680,000 ha being intended to supply industrial fibre. The annual establishment rate was 100,000 ha. By the year 2000, the plantation area was expected to be almost 2 million ha, of which 80% would be Pinus radiata.

Assessment of Effectiveness

Despite the massive rise in plantation area, many observers have questioned the importance of incentives in creating this outcome. The availability of incentives for forest plantations was a minor factor contributing to forest industry growth, once a critical initial mass of plantations was established. Subsidies had only a secondary impact in promoting plantations, with more important factors being a comparative advantage and a favorable general economic environment.

By 1994, there was evidence that the subsidies had served their purpose and were no longer necessary. At that time, many Chilean forest companies were foregoing the incentives to avoid government requirements, including long-term allocation of land to forestry and restrictions on the management and harvesting of the plantations. There was also widespread criticism that they favored large landowners and companies and that plantations were being created on natural forestland. Dasgupta et al. (1998) reported that the conversion of land and native forests to tree plantations had become an ecological problem.

A second reason why it is suggested that plantation establishment incentives were not required is that while many plantations were established on degraded lands, some have been established on prime agricultural land. This is evidence of the inherent profitability of plantations in Chile. Eucalyptus globulus and Pinus radiata plantations are both more profitable in Chile than the next best land use, cattle ranching, at all interest rates considered (i.e., between 2 to 20%). In contrast, in Brazil, a cattle ranching was more attractive than establishing Pinus taeda at discount rates of 12% and higher but was less attractive at interest rates of 8% or less. Eucalyptus grandis plantations were more profitable in Brazil at all interest rates.

Conversely, the reforestation incentive was "stunningly successful", creating one of the world's most competitive forest resources in a generation and supplying 95% of the fibre used by the domestic forest products industry. While subsidy payments are estimated to have totalled approximately US$50 million, the Chilean government achieved its purpose but may have paid more than necessary. The planting programme has been so successful that land prices have risen significantly and there is reputed to be less land remaining available for plantation establishment than in Brazil or Argentin. If imitation is an endorsement, then further evidence of the value placed on the successful outcome is provided by Colombia and Ecuador, which have adopted the Chilean model for their own incentive programmes.

India

Indian government has promulgated forest policy since the Arthasashtra Indica was issued in the third century B.C. The most recent National Forest Policy (NFP), passed in 1988, sets the highest priority on environmental protection. Its significance also lies in the formal recognition of communities as partners in forest management. Management planning shared by the state and local communities, or Joint Forest Management (JFM) was legalized in 1990.

The Federal Government has primary responsibility for forest management and most forests are under its control, but day-to-day tasks are overseen by the state forest departments. A small but increasing proportion of area is under site-specific Village Forest Management Plans developed through JFM. These incorporate management objectives and assign rights and responsibilities based on community-wide consultation. As of 1 January 2000, JFM has been implemented on more than 10.25 million hectares of degraded forests through 36,075 Village Forest Committees (India MoEF 2000).

The NFP remained consistent with its predecessor Act by maintaining a target of putting one-third of the national land area under forest. The country is far from meeting this target. Nearly 23% of the land base (76 million ha) is recorded as forest but only 19.5% (64 million ha) actually has tree cover (Ahmed 1997). Furthermore, 35% of the forest is badly degraded and the general trend is downwards, due to population and grazing pressures.

To achieve the target set in the NFP, roughly 33 million ha need to be afforested and 31 million ha of degraded and open forest need restocking, presuming no further deforestation. During the late 1990's, already low afforestation levels declined further, mainly due to funding reductions. In 1996-97, only 1.3 million ha were afforested, which was below the average of 1.5 million ha in previous three years. Of this, roughly one million ha or 70 per cent of plantation establishment was carried out by the State.

It was clear that the objectives of the new Forest Policy would not be achieved without a new investment strategy and so in 1999, the Government of India and the federal Ministry of Environment and Forests developed a National Forest Action Programme (NFAP). The NFAP outlines a 20-year forest management strategy, including a major afforestation programme and continued regeneration of degraded natural forests through JFM. A reforestation rate of 3 million ha/year is required for twenty years to meet the national forest area target.

Financial Incentive Programmes

The key incentive in the JFM programme is the sharing of benefits between the MoEF and participating communities. India established a National Afforestation and Eco-Development Board in 1992 to promote afforestation, tree-planting and ecological restoration. The majority of new planting is on public lands under the "20-point Programme for Afforestation", which provides free seedlings for planting on private lands. In addition, direct government planting continues.

There are other programmes that provide incentives for plantation establishment. A federally sponsored "Integrated Afforestation and Eco-Development Projects" Scheme was initiated in 1989-90 to fund local reforestation projects, especially on ecologically fragile watersheds in mountainous areas. To address problems related to seed sourcing and quality, a "Seed Development Scheme" was initiated. Under this programme, the federal government funds state government efforts to develop facilities for seed collection, testing, certification, storage and distribution.

Assessment of Effectiveness

To date, the impacts of the seed distribution and reforestation programmes have been undermined by widespread use of inappropriate and low quality seeds. This has led to plantation failures and poor growth, which in the long run will discourage forest establishment. Recent measures described above are intended to correct these problems. Where improved seed has been used, eucalyptus yields have been raised from 7 to 20 m^3/ha/year and superior clones of poplar are even more productive.

India is caught in a dilemma over timber pricing - higher prices make plantation establishment more attractive yet also increases pressure on existing forests. There is abundant unfulfilled domestic demand for wood since the forest products sector faces raw material shortages and operates well below its rated capacity. He estimated that 15% of the national timber harvest is consumed industrially, which is low relative to many other countries but still reflects the expansionary impacts of now discontinued policies that priced wood at very low rates and restricted imports. As of 1991, there were 276 mills producing paper and newsprint, pulp, plywood, and matches, as well as 23,000 sawmills. A variety of recent policy changes will cause a contraction of capacity. These include major reductions of import duties on wood products, particularly logs, a total ban on export of timber from India, a ban on harvesting in natural forests, and reductions in tariffs for forest products to make wood products more affordable.

The impacts of land reform policies on plantation investment are also mixed. While restrictions imposed by some states prohibit any individual or company from owning more than 20 ha, forest products companies are contracting with small farmers, through buy-back arrangements, to meet their requirements for timber. This provides a financial incentive for tree farming.

There are even broader issues. High population levels and poverty are the two main causes of destructive pressure on forests and meeting the needs of the rural poor and tribal people has been given high priority. The effectiveness of forest establishment incentives will depend on the rate at which these pressures continue and the government's assessment of priorities.

Indonesia

The utilisation and management of forests are governed by the Indonesian Constitution of 1945. All natural forests are owned and administered by the State, which may temporarily assign property rights (e.g. as a timber concession) or irrevocably transfer land to private parties. Forestry policies are linked to national development objectives defined under 25-year National

Development Plans. Indonesia is now in its second development plan, running from 1994 to 2019. These plans are subdivided into five-year economic plans (Repelitas). From Repelita I through IV (1969-1989), the long-term national goals were to increase forestry development and establish large-scale forest-based industries.

Aggressive exploitation is being replaced with emphasis on environmental protection and sustainable management. Repelita V (1989-1994) limited log extraction, froze the issuance of new mill licenses, increased reforestation taxes by 150%, added an export tax on sawn timber (which has forced inefficient mills to close), encouraged public participation and improved training and monitoring. Repelita VI (1995-1999) has more strongly emphasized sustainable forest management.

The Industrial Timber Estate (Hutan Tanaman Industri - HTI) development programme was initiated in 1983 to establish industrial timber plantations. These were intended to supply wood for the burgeoning forest products sector and to reduce pressure on natural forests (Potter and Lee 1998). Initially, there were separate HTI programmes for the pulp and plywood sectors. HTI agreement holders are granted 35-year concessions, which may be extended by another 35 years.

A critical aspect of forest planning is the categorization of the forest estate, which is the basis for designating areas for natural forest concessions (Hak Pengusahaan Hutan - HPH), timber plantation concessions, and tree crop plantations (e.g. oil palm). "Unproductive" production (natural) forestlands are designated as sites for the development of timber plantations under HTIs. "Unproductive" land is forest with a low available commercial species volume.

Financial Incentive Programmes

The government has offered companies willing to establish HTIs interest-free loans drawn from a reforestation fund supplied by a reforestation tax levied on HPH concessionaires. These loans cover 32.5% of establishment costs and must be repaid in seven years. The government has also supported companies borrowing establishment capital and has allowed some to further lower establishment costs by cooperating with a state forestry company. Other incentives include low land taxes and, critically, the right to cut and sell any remnant vegetation on concessions.

In 1992, to accelerate the establishment of plantations and at the same time provide employment for transmigrants, HTI-Trans was developed. Under this programme, the Government will provide 40% of the investment while the remaining 60% are contributed by the private sector in a joint venture.

The government's objective was to establish 1.8 million ha by 1995, 2.3 million ha by 2000 and 10.5 million ha by 2030 (Sunderlin and Resosudarmo 1996). By 1995, HTI development programmes had accepted proposals for 1.75 million hectares. Kartodihardjo and Supriono (2000) reported that as of June 1998, 4.7 million ha has been allocated to create HTI plantations. Indonesia's Ministry of Forests (1997) reported that HTI programmes are targeted to have achieved about 6.4 million ha TE by the year 2000.

Assessment of Effectiveness

Indonesia is successfully established as a world leader in tropical plywood production and has an emerging pulp and paper industry. However, it is unclear how much the HTI programme and associated incentives contributed to these achievements. Actual HTI planting rates are considerably less than expected. As of December 1995, only 520,000 ha of HTI timber plantations had been established. Between 1990 and July 1997, actual planting was only 23.1% of the planned level. These authors cite government reports that 320,000 ha were planted in 1996/97 and an additional 311,000 ha was planned for 1998/99. This may bring the total HTI area to 1.15 million ha by the year 2000.

There are 22 companies managing 1.2 million ha of HTI that have not taken advantage of the subsidy from the reforestation fund. The director of one of these companies stated that receiving subsidies from the Reforestation Fund requires inclusion of state-owned companies in corporate management, which raises management and other costs. Thus, at this time, the timber plantation subsidy has no real benefit for some companies because the transaction costs are excessive. However, this situation may reflect only the current strength of Indonesia's export market, and not the prior attractiveness of subsidies.

The HTI programme is also reported to have been abused by HTI proponents who harvested the remaining natural forest on their concessions but had no intention of establishing plantations afterwards. These proponents also apply for and receive funds for reforestation which, it is asserted, they divert to higher-yielding investments. This behaviour has contributed to the gap between planned and actual HTI area. On some HTI areas, which are supposedly unforested, there may be a substantial amount of natural forest remaining, which may be understated to authorities. On average, 22% of the total area managed as HTI was actually productive natural forest prior to its establishment. This suggests that on the 4.7 million ha allocated for HTI as of June 1998, 1 million ha of natural forest may be cleared and converted. Thus, the HTI programme can contribute to loss of the natural forest, which is precisely the opposite of what was intended. A further consequence of the gap between planned and actual HTI planting is that industrial users are being forced to draw on the natural forest for wood fibre that was supposed to have been produced by plantations.

A more basic reason why the HTI programme has missed its establishment targets is that even the subsidized returns from fast-growing plantations are relatively unattractive. The HTIs have never been regarded as financially feasible as independent and self-sufficient enterprises - even with fast growing species, HTIs do not produce a return for 5-8 years. In contrast, oil palm plantations are much more profitable and are also heavily subsidized. Between 1986 and 1997, the area under oil palm increased from 0.6 to 2.25 million ha. Since the economic crisis of 1997 increased the incentive to earn foreign exchange, oil palm development has accelerated. Thus, timber plantations cannot compete with other investments and are undermined by the government's oil palm subsidies.

Higher log prices would increase the financial attractiveness of timber plantations. Several factors dampen domestic log prices. One of these is the log export ban, recently reintroduced to help reduce illegal logging. Pervasive illegal logging is, itself, a second factor that suppresses prices. The World Bank (2000) reports that currently almost all domestic log consumption is met from illegal logging, with official concessions accounting only for processed exports. Timber supply is also inflated by other factors that increase harvesting pressure on the natural forest. Poor mapping and inventory work, and sometimes corruption, have led to encroachments by plantations in several conservation and protection areas, where a change in function was not permitted.

Poorly defined tenure is another factor that is beginning to reduce the attractiveness of timber plantation establishment. New plantations are being established in areas where local residents often have small plots and utilize the forest to obtain products. Some new HTIs have met resistance from local people who are being displaced. Thousands of farmers occupied an area licensed to one HTI company and cut trees, piled them at roadside and then sold them. The failure of another HTI company to keep a promise to build villagers a road, the commencement of work without consultation, intimidation by soldiers, and the felling of trees and high quality forest generated resentment that eventually led villagers to burn down the company's base camp and plantation. In response to these reactions, community forest schemes are being developed by HTIs as a compromise.

Due to macroeconomic events, foreign exchange earnings from processed timber exports, especially plywood, have to be maintained. To do this, the government feels compelled to emphasize plantation establishment to make up for shortfalls in wood supply due to degradation of the natural forest, disappointing rates of plantation development. The government has also counted on plantations to provide employment.

ASSESSMENT OF EFFECTIVENESS

Chile, India and Indonesia offer three contrasting examples of the usefulness and effectiveness of financial incentives for establishing plantations. Chile and Indonesia intended their plantations to supply fibre for an export-oriented forest products industry, which was also supported in its development. In both cases, powerful industrial sectors have been established, however the Indonesian industry depends heavily on the natural forest to provide domestic wood because plantation development has not been synchronized with industrial capacity growth. In contrast, India's main objectives for establishing plantations are providing ecological and social benefits associated with having a reasonable amount of healthy forests. Plantations are judged to be the fastest way to provide these benefits.

In all three countries, plantations were intended to take pressure off native forests, but they have so far been most successful in Chile in achieving this goal. In both India and Indonesia, plantation establishment has been inadequate to substantially reduce native timber use. Note that these two countries have the greatest population pressures, which suggests that it will require a disproportionately greater effort to relieve the pressure on the native forest.

Overall, the Chilean programme appears to have achieved its objectives while causing the least negative impacts. Because the opportunity costs are very difficult to calculate, it will be almost impossible to conclusively argue that the plantations and forest industries would have developed without subsidies. The Indonesian programme has been successful in the short-term, but the longer term outlook is uncertain due to the inability of plantations to satisfy combined industrial and personal demand. If the present level of pressure continues on the natural forest, there may be a timber shortage in the country unless wood prices rise in anticipation and stimulate an accelerated rate of plantation establishment. If wood prices rise too much, it will create problems for industry. The Indian programme appears to have been handicapped by poor quality seed and stock, and by insufficient technical capacity. However, these gaps are being addressed and an appropriate framework for longer term success appears to have been developed.

It is interesting that none of the subsidy programmes described above is widely viewed as a success. Brown (1999) astutely remarks that in most major plantation countries, the majority of plantation establishment has been carried out either by the government, or in tandem with government incentives. The evidence available from both Chile and Indonesia suggests that while timber plantation establishment may not require subsidies to entice investors today, the financial incentives played a major role in alerting investors to the potential of these investments. More importantly, simultaneous efforts to create a thriving forest products industry provided a long-term stimulus for plantation establishment that was initially necessary but is no longer so. While India's objectives differ somewhat from those of Chile and Indonesia, it is apparent that private sector funding will not provide adequate levels of plantation establishment. In that case, policies, which suppressed the prices paid by industry for timber, appear to have been a contributing factor.

One of the crucial differences between the Chilean and Indonesian experiences is that plantations are presently the highest yielding land use in many regions of Chile whereas oil palm is much more lucrative in Indonesia. Subsidies provided to oil palm growers further discouraged timber plantation development. It is important to support plantation development with policies that provide for a fair price for wood. This has not happened in Indonesia (due to high levels of illegal logging) or, until recently, in India (industrial timber prices were artificially suppressed). However, log exports into India remain restricted and wood product prices are reduced for consumers; both of these measures appear likely to depress wood prices. In contrast, Chile's plantation establishment programme was initiated at the same time that numerous market reforms were instituted, removing constraints on wood pricing. These reforms also created perceptions that the investment climate had become more favourable.

A second critical difference is that the Chilean government sold the land for plantations whereas Indonesia retained state ownership and there is even conflict between traditional rights and the rights of concessionaires. The uncertain tenure in Indonesia could not have helped persuade investors to establish timber plantations there. In contrast, rising land prices have provided a source of financial gain to Chilean plantation owners that few may have anticipated. Thirdly, the Chilean subsidies were more generous than those offered by Indonesia, which may also account for the greater level of success in the former country.

From a social perspective, the Indian incentives support efforts to create community-owned plantations. One of the shortcomings of the Chilean and Indonesian programmes is that they appear to have primarily benefited people and corporations who were already wealthy. While there is nothing wrong with supporting corporations per se, ignoring traditional land uses or customary rights is likely to lead to difficulties in the long-term, if not sooner. Indonesian plantation owners are already experiencing problems for this reason but are responding by offering joint ventures with local communities.

Conclusion

Financial incentives for plantation establishment have proven to be effective but they require supporting policies and conditions to be successful. In particular, secure tenure and other conditions that make the investment at least somewhat attractive without the subsidy are important. Adequate technical support is also required. Finally, the programme has to be sufficiently attractive if the uptake is to be sufficient to reduce pressure on native forests. Indeed, one measure of success appears to be a diminishing need for continued subsidization; Chile, as well as Australia and New Zealand, no longer offer extensive subsidies now that their forest industries are globally competitive.

Countries that are embarking on plantation incentive schemes intended to support industrial development now face strong competitors in the form of Chile, Indonesia and other countries that have already moved decisively into these areas. This suggests that future incentive programmes will either become more expensive if they are organized along traditional lines, or they will have to be modified in order to make them successful. Many countries, including Indonesia, are redirecting their assistance programmes to small scale and community level forestry. The use of direct government subsidies is becoming less desirable and privatization is now viewed as an essential part of economic development. Indirect incentives such as support for research, training, extension and possibly providing market information may be where government can make cost-effective contributions to promote privately funded forestation. Crossley et al. (1997) examined more innovative financing proposals, including the creation and development of entirely new financing mechanisms and instruments such as debt-for-nature swaps. These authors suggested that financial innovation might encompass the adaptation and application of well-established financial vehicles, such as bonds, to emerging investment areas such as sustainable forest management, biological diversity protection and conservation.

The foregoing has paid slight attention to beneficial externalities, which can be very valuable and are likely to increase in value over time. For example, Haltia and Keipi (1997) calculated that the ecological benefits (carbon sequestration and watershed protection) of Eucalyptus globulus and Pinus radiata plantations in Chile were $US 451/ha and $US 510/ha, respectively. Until markets develop for these types of benefits and private interests are able to capture some of their value (or internalize them, as is the case with community forests), creating a supply of external ecological and social benefits will be the major justification for providing financial incentives for plantation establishment.

IMPLICATIONS OF THE KYOTO PROTOCOL FOR PLANTATION DEVELOPMENT

Introduction

Since the adoption of the Kyoto Protocol in December 1997 by Parties to the United Nations Framework Convention on Climate Change (UNFCCC) there has been growing interest in Australia and internationally about the role carbon sequestration activities (sinks) may play in assisting countries to meet greenhouse gas emissions targets. Article 3.3 of the Protocol allows for net changes in greenhouse gas emissions from sources and removal by sinks due to afforestation, reforestation or deforestation since 1990 to be used in meeting emission reduction commitments. The Protocol also provides for emissions trading and credits generated by the sequestration of carbon in plantation forests may also become available for sale within an emissions trading market. This has created expectations of an increased investment funding for forest plantations as greenhouse gas emissions offsets but, to date, this investment has been relatively limited. International negotiations on greenhouse sinks and emissions trading under the Kyoto Protocol are at a critical stage with major decisions expected for the sixth Conference of the Parties (COP6) in The Hague in November 2000.

In Australia, the area of forest plantations is currently expanding rapidly, largely to meet expected future demand for wood products, with carbon offset investment currently only a minor driver. However, Australia is at the forefront of forest carbon related investment developments, and this experience provides some examples of alternative approaches that might be applied for this activity. In order for the Kyoto Protocol to act as a driver for the international trade of carbon credits, issues such as risk, measurement and verification, and the environmental and social implications of large scale revegetation will probably need to be addressed. This paper discusses the background to these issues and their implications for plantation development in Australia.

International Situation

The Kyoto Protocol was adopted after a protracted series of negotiations by Parties to the UNFCCC in 1997. Under the Protocol, these countries commit themselves to an aspirational target of reducing emissions of greenhouse gas by at least 5.2 percent below 1990 levels in the first commitment period (2008-2012). Emission reduction targets are differentiated between countries, for example Australia's target allows for an 8 percent increase over 1990 emission levels compared with projected increases under a business-as-usual scenario of around 40 percent.

Vegetation plays an important role in global cycling of carbon dioxide CO_2 (Fig. 11.1). Large amounts of CO_2 are exchanged annually between terrestrial vegetation and associated carbon pools (such as litter and organic soil carbon). CO2 is

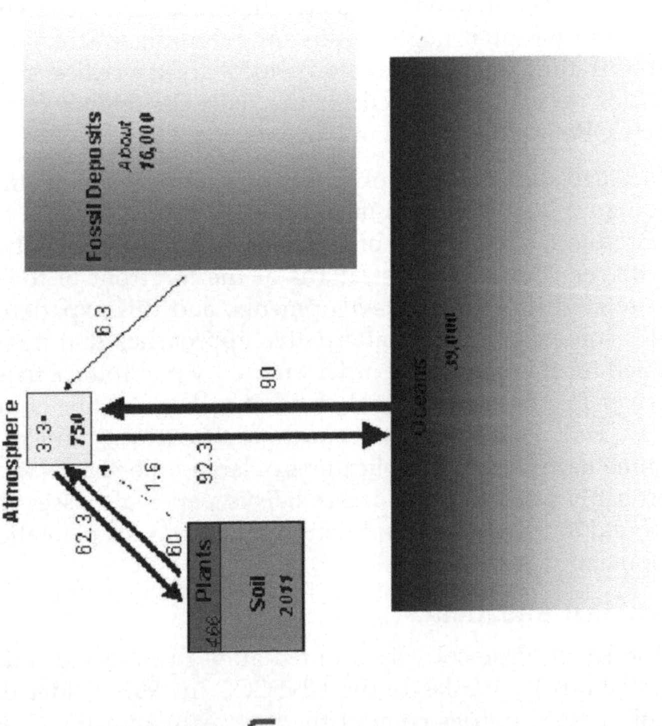

Fig. 11.1: Global Cycling of Carbon dioxide

absorbed by plants in the process of photosynthesis. Some of this carbon is stored in the plant, and some is released during respiration and decomposition of plant remains.

During negotiation of the Kyoto Protocol a number of concerns were raised about the inclusion of vegetation sinks including:

- concern that countries would try to use action to enhance sinks as a way of avoiding action to reduce emissions in their energy and transport sectors;
- uncertainties in measuring emissions and sequestrations from vegetation;
- concerns that sequestration in carbon sinks is potentially reversible; and
- the possible impedance to economic development of some developing countries who argued they needed to continue conversion of some forest areas to satisfy the food production and other economic and social requirements of growing populations.

Inclusion of vegetation was supported because it offered important options for flexible, low-cost abatement of greenhouse gasses and was in line with the UNFCCC requirement to preserve and enhance sinks. At Kyoto, pro-sinks countries argued that unless sinks were included in the Protocol, there would be little incentive for countries to improve methodologies to measure them, and no requirement for countries to take action to reduce emissions from loss of sinks. There was also recognition of the importance of sink activity in the global carbon cycle and a belief inclusion would help to stem the ongoing loss of forests in some countries.

Final agreement resulted in the inclusion in the Protocol of the limited set of sink activities set out in Article 3.3 and continued negotiation over the inclusion of additional sink activities under Article 3.4. Enhancing carbon storage in vegetation through sustainable forest and vegetation management is now an important part of greenhouse response for a number of countries, including Australia (Commonwealth of Australia 1998).

The Protocol provides for trading of emission reduction units between parties and for joint emission reduction and sink enhancement projects between developed countries through Joint Implementation (JI) and between developed and developing countries through the Clean Development Mechanism (CDM), although the rules about how these mechanisms will operate are still to be negotiated. It has been argued that emission reduction units should be fully 'fungible' and that CO_2 sequestered in vegetation (a carbon credit) is directly equivalent to CO_2 emissions from fossil fuel burning. Whether vegetation-related projects will be included in the CDM is still to be decided, but a number of pilot projects have been conducted to gather experience in this area. One key difference between CDM and JI or other emissions trading activities is that credits from CDM and JI projects undertaken from the year 2000 onwards can be used to assist in achieving compliance in the first commitment period.

Substantive international negotiations on sinks issues were effectively on hold until finalization of the Special Report on Land Use, Land Use Change and Forestry prepared by the Intergovernmental Panel on Climate Change in May 2000 (Watson et al. 2000). Decisions on major issues in sinks, mechanisms (such as emissions trading and the CDM) compliance and reporting are expected for the sixth Conference of the Parties in November 2000. For sinks, these include definitions of forest, afforestation, reforestation and deforestation under Articles 3.3, the inclusion of additional activities under Article 3.4, and progress on measurement and accounting issues for the land use change and forestry sector.

Factors Shaping the Market for Carbon Credits

The market price for carbon credits will depend on demand and supply, and the nature of an emissions trading market. The potential for carbon credits from plantations to compete against alternative abatement options will depend on the cost of generating plantation-based credits. Key factors in determining this cost are the extent, availability and cost of suitable land, tree growth rates, commercial and legal infrastructure arrangements and the nature of supportive government policies, risk factors and transaction costs associated with selling carbon credits.

Cost of Plantation Based Carbon Credits Relative to Other Abatement Options

The cost of carbon credits from a forest plantation is a function of land price, establishment and maintenance costs, the cost of borrowing funds for establishment, transaction costs associated with trading carbon credits for forestry acts, revenues from other products and carbon accumulation rates. Plantations accumulate carbon at an average rate of 0.4 to 8 tonnes ha^{-1} yr^{-1} over a rotation length or until mean annual increment peaks. This rate varies with site and climatic conditions, species and management inputs. Forest plantations can be managed for conservation or production purposes. Those managed for production of wood products or carbon, generally receive high management inputs, and often yields have been improved through tree breeding or silvicultural research. For conservation forests management inputs will generally be lower, and growth is likely to be slower. If these conservation forests are maintained in perpetuity and natural regeneration processes can be re-established, the amount of carbon stored on the site can remain at an equilibrium level. In forests harvested for wood production, the storage is temporary and carbon is released during harvest and subsequent decay of detritus or wood products. If a larger forest estate is managed on a sustainable basis, the overall pool of carbon will remain higher than that previously available in a series of separate plantings. An estate manager may prefer to trade the carbon accumulating in this pool rather than trade the carbon in an individual stand.

There are a number of factors that will influence the cost of growing plantations for carbon credits, including land costs, establishment and maintenance costs and whether the plantation is grown to supply products other than carbon credits. The effect of these factors on the cost of supplying carbon credits from plantations can result in a wide range of cost estimates. Several studies have attempted to estimate the cost of supplying a tonne of carbon from plantations established purely for carbon credits. These estimates vary widely, ranging between A$3.09 to A$92.66 per tonne of carbon. However, comparison across these studies is difficult because assumptions for land value, establishment costs, species and purpose vary.

Various models have been used to estimate the costs of other abatement options. These studies have simulated carbon equivalent permit prices in 2010 under various Kyoto-consistent scenarios, ranging from A$36 to A$403 per tonne of carbon1, assuming competitive trading of emission permits between Annex B developed countries.

Due to the 'land linked' nature of plantations, as demand for carbon sequestered from plantation increases, the marginal cost of plantation development will increase, due to increased land and other plantation costs. This increase will result in the price of carbon sequestered by plantations increasing until it equates with the cost of carbon reductions through other abatement options. In cases where the value of carbon does not reach a level to cover all costs associated with sequestering carbon in vegetation, investments will depend on supplementary returns from other products such as wood, or possible subsidy by government for environmental, industrial or regional development purposes.

Global Potential for Plantation Offsets

There have been a number of estimates on the area potentially available for future forest plantations that could contribute to carbon sequestration. Estimates have generally been constrained by the quality of biophysical data. It is estimated that 420-450 million hectares (encompassing degraded drylands and deforested watersheds and the most degraded forest fallows) could be available for afforestation worldwide. However, even without consideration of other physical requirements for growing plantations (such as climate, rainfall and soil), expansion of plantations for carbon credits is likely to be constrained by the social and political factors which define current land use. It is suggested that maintaining existing forests and increasing the area under forest vegetation could absorb the equivalent of 12-15 per cent of future greenhouse gas emissions.

Recent estimates suggest that carbon stocks in developed countries could increase by 7 to 46 Mt C yr^{-1} due to afforestation and reforestation after 1990 (using the 'IPCC' definition) in the first commitment period of the Protocol. Estimates of the global sequestration potential are between 197 to 584 Mt C yr^{-1} (Watson et al. 2000). In comparison, reduction in carbon stock due to deforestation is about 90 Mt C yr^{-1} in developed countries and 1788 Mt C yr^{-1} globally. These estimates cover a wide range with uncertainty about growth rates and about reported rates of plantation establishment, but indicate the current losses due to deforestation are much greater than potential gains from afforestation or reforestation.

Accounting for Carbon Credits

Traditionally forest inventory has focused on obtaining estimates of timber volume in the bole of the tree. Carbon generally makes up about 50 percent of the mass of most plant material, and carbon is estimated from an inventory of total biomass. In plantations this requires assessment of the biomass stored in other components of an ecosystem, including:

- stems, branches, leaves and roots of the living trees and understorey vegetation;
- dead coarse (woody) and fine litter in the forest floor; and
- highly decomposed and transformed plant material incorporated within the mineral soil, generally described as soil organic matter.

The rate of accumulation of carbon in a plantation established on cleared land generally follows a logistic (sigmoidal) curve, with initial emissions from soils following establishment, slow initial growth, more rapid accumulation after the site is occupied followed by a decline as the trees mature. Changes in carbon stocks in vegetation and soil removed or affected by plantation establishment need to be accounted. Reduction in carbon stocks due to harvest or other natural disturbances will also need to be accounted. Ongoing storage of carbon in wood products can only be accounted to a limited extent because of the IPCC inventory rules required under Article 5.2 of the Kyoto Protocol.

Plantation Development in Australia

The total commercial forest plantation estate at the end of 1999 was 1,337,000 ha (Wood and Allison 2000). Of this, an estimated 328,000 ha established since 1990 is considered compliant with the current IPCC definition of reforestation. Based on the analysis, there is an estimated 18.5 million hectares of cleared agricultural land in Australia with sufficient rainfall to grow commercial timber plantations. Other studies suggest a smaller area is biologically suitable. Only a proportion of this land is likely to shift from agricultural to forest-based uses, with the change depending on management decisions of individual landowners. It is suggested that just over 1 million hectares is both biologically and economically suitable for plantation establishment, based on comparative financial returns to land owners and assumed industry development options.

The rate of plantation establishment has risen rapidly in the last five years, from 30,000 ha^{-1} yr^{-1} in 1995 to almost 95,000 ha^{-1} yr^{-1} in 1999. Future rates of planting are uncertain but Commonwealth and State governments have collectively agreed to a goal of trebling the plantation area to 3 million hectares by 2020. This would result in almost 2 million hectares of new plantations since 1990.

Drivers of Plantation Development

Direct government investment, other policy actions, and private investment, are the main drivers of plantation development in Australia. Government policy has been a significant factor in plantation development since the 1960s. Most of the plantation estate planted prior to 1995 was established directly by governments or with government funding assistance. However, direct government investment in plantation establishment is now relatively low. Governments now aim to facilitate expansion of state plantations in other ways, such as joint ventures with private landowners, taxation incentives, loans at subsidised rates or grants. Governments continue to play a significant role in setting an institutional framework that allows for the development of an efficient plantation sector and competitive markets for plantation based products. Other government policies and initiatives that influence Australia's competitiveness in the establishment of plantations and the supply of plantation based carbon credits are listed in Table 11.1 and Table 11.2.

Table 11.1: Government initiatives influenced plantations and carbon sinks in Australia

Policy/Initiative	Description
National Forest Policy Statement (1992)	Main mechanism to ensure the sustainable use, conservation and enhancement of forests. Objectives include the maintenance of the native forest estate and the further establishment of forestry plantations on cleared land. It also highlights the need to manage forests to maintain or increase their net carbon sink and storage capacity, and to minimize the emission of greenhouse gases from forest activities.
Farm Forestry Programme (1993)	Commonwealth and State Government initiative aimed at encouraging the incorporation of commercial tree growing and management into farming systems for the purpose of wood and non-wood production, increasing agricultural productivity and sustainable natural resource management.
Plantations for Australia: the 2020 Vision (1997)	Partnership between the Commonwealth, State and industry to build a sustainable, commercially orientated and internationally competitive industry by creating an environment that will attract private investment. The partnership envisages a trebling of the area of Australia's plantation estate by 2020 by establishing an average of 80000 ha of additional plantations a year or a total of 2 million ha.
Bushcare: the National Vegetation Initiative (1998)	Aims to expand revegetation activities and reverse the long term decline in the quality and extent of Australia's native vegetation through joint work by governments, industries and communities. A major component of the Natural Heritage Trust (NHT).

(Contd…)

Policy/Initiative	Description
Bush for Greenhouse (1998)	Aims to promote investment into the establishment of greenhouse sinks, in particular, by facilitating corporate funding of revegetation projects. Companies investing in the programme will be able to obtain recognition for the carbon sequestered, thus at least nationally offsetting emissions from other activities.
National Greenhouse Strategy (1998)	Based on National Greenhouse Response Strategy (1992), the Commonwealth and State governments in partnership with the Australian Local Government Association have developed a policy framework for advancing Australia's domestic greenhouse response into the next century. Activities include the launching of new measures to increase greenhouse emission reduction activities and to integrate greenhouse into other major policy initiatives such as the NHT. Goals are to limit net greenhouse gas emissions, in particular to meet Australia's International commitments; to foster knowledge and understanding of greenhouse issues; and to lay the foundations for adaptation to climate change. It includes actions to enhance greenhouse sinks and encourage sustainable forestry and vegetation management.
Carbon Rights Legislation Amendment Act 1998 (NSW)	This amends the Conveyancing Act 1919, the Electricity (Pacific Power) Act 1950, the Energy Services Corporations Act 1995 and the Forestry Act 1916 of NSW. It recognises carbon sequestration in forests planted on cleared land since 1990 and allows legal rights to be established to that sequestration. It further allows corporations in the Electricity business to buy, own and sell such right, and also empowers State Forests of NSW to own, sell and manage these rights on its own behalf or for investing persons or corporations. The Act does not establish a carbon trading system, providing only legal recognition of the ownership and trade of carbon rights.

(Contd…)

Policy/Initiative	Description
Replanting Victoria 2020 (1999)	Aims to increase areas of carbon sinks, through revegetation projects, reforestation projects, and plantation projects. The plantation component will develop greenhouse demonstration plantations around the State and landowners can apply for assistance in setting up greenhouse plantations. A carbon tracking system to record, track and audit the performance of carbon sinks is also being developed.

Table 11.2: Recent policy initiatives specifically aimed at facilitating carbon related investments

Policy/Initiative	Description
(Bush for (Greenhouse (1998)	Aims to promote investment into the establishment of greenhouse sinks, in particular, by facilitating corporate funding of revegetation projects. Companies investing in the programme will be able to obtain recognition for the carbon sequestered, thus at least notionally offsetting emissions from other activities.
National Greenhouse Strategy (1998)	(Based on National Greenhouse Response Strategy (1992), the Commonwealth and State governments in partnership with the Australian Local Government Association have developed a policy framework for (advancing Australia's domestic greenhouse response into the next century. Activities include the launching of new measures to increase greenhouse remission reduction activities and to integrate greenhouse into other major policy initiatives such as the NHT. Goals are to limit net greenhouse gas emissions, in particular to meet Australia's international commitments; to foster knowledge and understanding of greenhouse issues; and to lay the foundations for adaptation to climate change. It includes actions to enhance greenhouse sinks and encourage sustainable forestry and vegetation management.
Carbon Rights Legislation Amendment Act 1998 (NSW)	This amends the Conveyancing Act 1919, the Electricity (Pacific Power) Act 1950, the Energy Services Corporations Act 1995 and the Forestry Act M916 of NSW. It recognizes carbon sequestration in forests planted on cleared land since 1990 and allows legal rights to be established to that sequestration. It further allows corporations in the Electricity business to buy, own and sell such right, and also empowers State Forests of NSW to own, sell and manage these rights on its own behalf or for investing persons or corporations. The Act does not establish a carbon trading system, providing only legal recognition of the ownership and trade of carbon rights.

(Contd…)

Policy/Initiative	Description
Replanting Victoria 2020 (1999)	Aims to increase areas of carbon sinks, through revegetation projects, reforestation projects, and plantation projects. The plantation component will develop greenhouse demonstration plantations around the State and landowners can apply for assistance in setting up greenhouse plantations. A carbon tracking system to record, track and audit the performance of carbon sinks is also being developed.

Private Investment

Recent expansion of the plantation estate has largely been financed by private investment. Direct investment by larger foreign companies has occurred in Western Australia, Tasmania, the Murray Valley, and the Green Triangle area of South Australia and Victoria. Smaller Australian based investment companies have also become active in plantation establishment, using funding from private investors to purchase or rent cleared agricultural land to develop plantations. These have largely been short rotation hardwood plantations to produce product for sale in the international pulpwood market.

To meet the '2020 Vision' target estate of three million hectares the following conditions would need to be satisfied:

- Continued flow of private investment.
- Maintained global demand for timber products particularly in the Asian region.
- Maintenance of positive Federal, State and local government policies on plantation development.
- Maintenance and expansion of current levels of government investment in plantations for industry development or environmental benefits.
- Development of market mechanisms for carbon offsets and emissions trading.

Environmental benefits may also become a significant new driver for government or private investments. For example, increasing dryland and stream salinity resulting from past deforestation and current farming practices could affect significant areas in Australia. Establishment of plantations to restore the hydrological balance in recharge areas catchments at risk is proposed as a partial solution to this problem. However, much of the land that is likely to produce salinity benefits from plantation establishment is in lower rainfall, lower productivity areas where traditional pine and eucalypt species perform poorly. Therefore, new species and alternate options for plantation management may be required if this development is to become a reality.

Carbon As a Driver in Plantation Development

Australia is leading the development and implementation of institutional and legal mechanisms aimed at allowing efficient trade in carbon credits. Some government programmes are indicated in Table 11.1. NSW State Forests have been particularly active. After negotiation of the Kyoto Protocol, this state-owned forest management agency decided to become an innovator in the area of climate change business opportunities. As a learning exercise, a financial trade was undertaken with Pacific Power (also a state owned corporation) purchasing the rights to carbon being sequestered in 1,000 ha of new planted forests, initially for one year, and subsequently for ten years. Concurrently, another trade was set up with Delta Electricity, where the right of State Forests to grow trees on land owned by Delta was exchanged for the rights to the carbon sequestered during the rotation. These trades were based on independent verification, including confirmation that the land was non-forested at the time of plantation establishment and assessment of the methods used for estimating carbon sequestration.

As a result of these initial trades, it was determined that legislation by the New South Wales government would be beneficial to the further legal recognition of carbon offsets and future establishment of carbon offset trading. Accordingly, the Carbon Rights Legislation Amendment Act was passed by the NSW Parliament in November 1998. This Act includes amendments to the Conveyancing Act, the Electricity (Pacific Power) Act, the Energy Services Corporations Act and the Forestry Act.

Under this arrangement, NSW State Forests has designed investment packages combining carbon sequestration and timber production. In February 2000, the Tokyo Electric Power Company signed a contract for the carbon rights to 40,000 ha of new plantations over the next decade. Plantation growers in other states, such as North Forest Products in Tasmania, the Western Australia Department of Conservation and Land Management, and Greenfield Resources Options and the Queensland Government have entered into arrangement for plantations carbon rights with petroleum producers or energy generators.

The 'Replanting Victoria' programme provides a different model, with the Victorian Government providing a subsidy of A$600 per hectare to small scale plantation growers in return for the rights to carbon sequestered in the plantations. This could be an effective way for government to foster plantation development for regional development or environmental benefits and reduce the transaction costs associated with carbon measurement in small-scale planting.

In 1999, the Sydney Futures Exchange began developing a new product based on increased carbon stocks in post-1990 forests. The SFE initiative was the result of a perceived market demand for risk management products to hedge the effects of the Kyoto Protocol. Trading carbon sequestration credits (CSC's) could help companies manage future permit price uncertainties by enabling them to trade future credits at a price agreed at the time of trade. Suppliers of carbon to the market will have to use an agreed standard and adhere to the conditions of a carbon deed. This Deed included requirements to have in place appropriate risk management, including insurance and demonstration of sound prudential assets and financial liquidity.

Potential benefits from this early trading in sinks included:

- Providing for early risk management;
- Realization of the potential for vegetation sinks as a low cost emissions abatement option and in providing other environmental benefits;
- Providing early price discovery; and
- Demonstration that financial market participants can make an emissions trading system work.

Recently the SFE decided not to proceed with the development of this product, but other significant market activity is developing in this area.

Issues Requiring Resolution for Carbon to be a Significant Driver in Plantation Development

Risks

Institutional and natural risks will affect decisions to invest in plantations for carbon credits. Major institutional risks include ratification of the Kyoto Protocol and associated decisions regarding the inclusion of sinks and their potential contribution to emission reduction targets. Shifts in the price of carbon also represent a risk; particularly to small growers who may sell carbon credits in one market, but have to purchase them in another when they intend to harvest for timber. There are also risks related to shifts in government policies such as pricing and allocation policies for timber, plantation related regulations such as environmental requirements and forest ownership rights, and taxation provisions. All these sources of risk could add to transaction costs. Natural risks include drought, pests, or fire.

Risks might be covered in a sales contract but this may add to transaction costs. For instance, a buyer may want compensation for the loss of the carbon credit if a fire occurs or if carbon credit regulations change. Financial risks in developing plantations for carbon credits can be hedged if the plantations also produce wood products. Most plantations have been developed to supply wood products with the creation of carbon credits as a potential additional benefit, but some investments are occurring with the creation of carbon credits as a primary financial driver. Risk could also be managed through the formation of carbon 'pool managers' who keep a certain proportion of stored carbon in reserve to allow for losses associated with unforeseen circumstances.

Transactions Costs

Marketing and selling a product involves transaction costs. For carbon credits derived from plantations, transaction costs include the costs associated with measuring, verifying and certifying the carbon sequestered. Depending on the nature of the market, transaction costs can be borne by the buyer or seller.

Transactions costs will raise the costs (and lower the benefit) to each participant in the trade, and reduce the volume of exchanges. As there have been few sales of plantation based carbon credits the cost of marketing and selling carbon credits is largely unknown, and it is difficult to compare the transaction costs associated with plantation based carbon credits with other forms of carbon credits or abatement options. Transaction costs will be determined in part by the rules and regulations established for certifying, verifying and trading credits and other costs associated with accessing and trading in an emissions trading market. In the case of the CDM and possibly for the other mechanisms, there may be other costs, such as the proposed 'adaptation tax' on CDM projects which could also affect the volume of trade.

Measurement and Verification Issues

All plantation based carbon sequestration activities will require monitoring systems that enable quantification and independent verification of carbon stock changes. Measurement standards and requirements for both national and project level accounting are still to be decided. Annex 1 Parties generally have the basic technical capacity to measure carbon stocks and net greenhouse gas emissions in terrestrial ecosystems. However, few if any, countries perform all these measurements routinely, particularly soil inventories. Most countries are likely to adopt a combination of modeling and direct measurement as part of a comprehensive accounting system. Uncertainty in measurement could be dealt with by extending the application of good practice guidance that has been developed by the IPCC for other inventory categories (Watson et al. 2000). For plantation projects developed under joint implementation or the CDM, other issues need to be addressed (Brown et al. 2000). For example, a project would need to demonstrate that increased carbon storage resulting from the project is additional to that which would occur with out it, and a baseline would need to be developed to quantify these additional sequestration benefits.

Social and Community Concerns

A variety of concerns have been raised relating to social and economic impacts of plantation based carbon-offsets projects on smaller rural communities, and the environmental implications of large scale forestation projects (Bass et al. 2000).

Concerns for rural communities include impeding or removing access to land for traditional uses and sources of livelihood for rural communities, and the inability of small community-based projects to compete with large-scale reforestation activities. In Australia, communities are also reacting to the rapid expansion of plantations onto agricultural land, and perceived impacts on community structure and employment. However, this structural adjustment is occurring for a range of reasons and the reality is that the proportion of agricultural land in Australia that is likely to be converted to forest plantations is relatively small. For example, in Australia the national target is 2 million hectares of new plantation by 2020 compared with 18 million hectares of agricultural land that is potentially suitable.

Article 12 of the Kyoto Protocol states that projects under the Clean Development Mechanism shall be used to assist developing country parties in achieving sustainable development. However, individual host countries are likely to be best placed to assess whether prospective CDM projects will assist them with sustainable development. Other solutions to potential community impacts include social and environmental impact assessment of projects, providing incentives for projects with multiple benefits, and reducing transaction costs for community based projects (CIFOR 2000). In general, as the area of plantations increases, there are likely to be increasing political limitations placed on the use of agricultural land for plantation development. Economic considerations such as the ability of plantation forestry to provide a return not less than that from competing land uses will also constrain plantation expansion.

Environmental Concerns

Concerns have been raised about the potential impacts of forestation on water yield and quality, biodiversity. For example, increasing water utilisation by trees in new plantations may have unintended consequences, such as reduction in downstream water flows and decreased aquifer recharge. Therefore, while plantations have the potential to provide significant salinity or other water quality benefits, reductions in flow may result in increased salt concentrations in streams and reduced water availability to irrigators. This will require careful planning of plantation location based on a sound understanding of landscape topography, soils and hydrology.

Biodiversity impacts of plantations can be moderated by using native species where possible, retaining and enhancing areas of native vegetation within the plantation development, and incorporating more compositional and structural diversity in the plantation by maintaining a mix of age classes and plantation species.

Conclusion

The Kyoto Protocol, including its provisions for emissions trading and other market-based mechanisms for carbon trading, represents a considerable opportunity for increased private sector funding for plantation development and improved forest management. Governments will need to be strategic in securing maximum benefit from these developments and effectively integrating them into policies and programmes to meet domestic industry, regional development and environmental objectives. However, potential sellers of carbon credits will need to take into account risks associated with trading carbon and governments will need to address community and environmental concerns about large scale plantation development. There is an ongoing need for national and international research in greenhouse science, carbon cycling in vegetation, measurement of carbon stocks and social and economic implications of greenhouse gas abatement options.

12

Prehistoric Plants

ARCHAEOPTERIS

Archaeopteris is an extinct genus of tree-like plants with fern-like leaves. A useful index fossil, this tree is found in strata dating from the Upper Devonian to Lower Carboniferous, and has a global distribution.

Until the recent discovery of Wattieza, many scientists considered Archaeopteris to be the earliest known tree. Bearing buds, reinforced branch joints, and branched trunks similar to today's timber, it is more reminiscent of modern seed-bearing trees than other spore bearing taxa; It combines characteristics of woody trees and herbaceous ferns, and belongs to a group of extinct plants sometimes called the progymnosperms, plants with gymnosperm-like wood but that produce spores rather than seeds.

Anatomy

The trees of this genus were small to medium in size with leafy foliage reminiscent of some conifers. The large fronds were thickly set with fan-shaped leaflets on stems that inclined sharply upward. They typically grew to 10 m in height. Some species are large, with trunks that exceeded 1.5 m in diameter. The veining branches diverged dichotomously. There was also intermediate feathering at each frond node or axes.

Leafy shoots occurred in opposite arrangement in a single plane. The leaflets, or pinnules, overlapped one another and were subcircular to wedge-shaped. On fertile branches, the leaves were replaced by spore capsules.

Aside from its woody trunk, Archaeopteris possessed other modern adaptations to light interception and perhaps to seasonality as well. The large umbrella of fronds seems to have been quite optimized for light interception at the canopy level. In some species, the pinnules were shaped and oriented to avoid shading one another. There is evidence that whole fronds were shed together as single units, perhaps seasonally like modern deciduous foliage or like trees in the cypress family Cupressaceae.

The plant had nodal zones that would have been important sites for the subsequent development of lateral roots and branches. Some branches were latent and adventitious, similar to those produced by living trees that eventually develop into roots. Before this time, shallow, rhizomatous roots had been the norm, but with Archaeopteris, deeper root systems were being developed that could support ever higher growth.

Habitat

Evidence indicates that Archaeopteris preferred wet soils, growing close to river systems and in flood plain woodlands. It would have formed a significant part of the canopy vegetation of early forests. Speaking of the first appearance of Archaeopteris on the world-scene, Stephen Scheckler, a professor of biology and geological sciences at Virginia Polytechnic Institute, says, "When [Archaeopteris] appears, it very quickly became the dominant tree all over the Earth. On all of the land areas that were habitable, they all had this tree".

Scheckler goes on to say, "Its litter fed the streams and was a major factor in the evolution of freshwater fishes, whose numbers and varieties exploded in that time, and influenced the evolution of other marine ecosystems. It was the first plant to produce an extensive root system, so had a profound impact on soil chemistry. And once these ecosystem changes happened, they were changed for all time. It was a one-time thing".

Looking roughly like a top-heavy Christmas tree, Archaeopteris may have played a part in the transformation of Earth's climate during the Devonian before becoming extinct within a short period of time at the beginning of the Carboniferous period.

Relationship to Conifers

Because Archaeopteris reproduced by releasing spores rather than by producing seeds, paleobotanists suspect that modern trees come from a sibling line of plants they call the "progymnosperms". Archaeopteris is more like an ancient cousin than a direct ancestor.

Discovery and Classification

Archaeopteris was originally classified as a fern, and it remained classified so for over 100 years. In 1911, Russian paleontologist Mikhail Dimitrievich Zalessky described a new type of petrified wood from the Donetz Basin in Russia. He called the wood Callixylon, though he did not find any structures other than the trunk. The similarity to conifer wood was recognized. It was also noted that ferns of the genus Archaeopteris were often found associated with fossils of Callixylon.

In the 1960s, paleontologist Charles B. Beck was able to demonstrate that the fossil wood known as Callixylon and the leaves known as Archaeopteris were actually part of the same plant It was a plant with a mixture of characteristics not seen in any living plant, a link between true gymnosperms and ferns.

The genus Archaeopteris is placed in the order Archaeopteridales and family Archaeopteridaceae. The name is similar to that of the first known feathered bird, Archaeopteryx, but in this case refers to the feather-like nature of the plant's fronds.

CALAMITES

Calamites is a genus of extinct arborescent (tree-like) horsetails to which the modern horsetails (genus Equisetum) are closely related. Unlike their herbaceous modern cousins, these plants were medium-sized trees, growing to heights of more than

30 metres (100 feet). They were components of the understories of coal swamps of the Carboniferous period.

Taphonomy

A number of organ taxa have been identified as part of a united organism, which has inherited the name Calamites in popular culture. Calamites correctly refers only to casts of the stem of Carboniferous/Permian sphenophytes, and as such is a form genus of little taxonomic value. There are two forms of casts, which can give mistaken impressions of the organims. The most common is an internal cast of the hollow (or pith-filled) void in the centre of the trunk. This can cause some confusion: firstly, it must be remembered that a fossil was probably surrounded with 4-5 times its width in (unpreserved) vascular tissue, so the organisms were much wider than the internal casts preserved. Further, the fossil gets narrower as it attaches to a rhizoid, a place where one would expect there to be the highest concentration of vascular tissue (as this is where the peak transport occurs). However, because the fossil is a cast, the narrowing in fact represents a constriction of the cavity, into which vascular tubes encroach as they widen.

Further organ genera belonging to sphenophytes include Arthropitys (stems which are preserved in a mineralised form), Astromyelon (permineralised rhizomes, distinguished from Arthropitys by the absence of a carinal canal), Annularia and Asterophylites (form genera of leaf-whorls which are embarrassingly paraphyletic).

Anatomy

The trunks of Calamites had a distinctive segmented, bamboo-like appearance and vertical ribbing. The branches, leaves and cones were all borne in whorls. The leaves were needle-shaped, with up to 25 per whorl.

Their trunks produced secondary xylem, meaning they were made of wood. The vascular cambium of Calamites was unifacial, producing secondary xylem towards the stem center, but not secondary phloem.

The stems of modern horsetails are typically hollow or contain numerous elongated air-filled sacs. Calamites was similar in that its trunk and stems were hollow, like wooden tubes. When these trunks buckled and broke, they could fill with sediment. This is the reason pith casts of the inside of Calamites stems are so common as fossils.

Reproduction

Calamites reproduced by means of spores, which were produced in small sacs organized into cones. They are also known to have possessed massive, underground rhizomes, which allowed for the production of clones of one tree. This is the only group of trees of their period known to have a clonal habit. This type of asexual reproduction would allow them to spread quickly into new territory, in addition to aiding in anchoring them firmly in the unstable ground along rivers and in newly deposited delta sediments. The rhizomes of Calamites look quite similar to the stems in most cases, but have nodes that get progressively closer together as they get out approach the apical area (the growth tip that spreads outward through the soil).

Different Forms

Calamites come in a variety of different "form genera". One type, Calamites *suckowi*, is distinguishable from other Calamites forms by its prominent, swollen nodes and relatively wide-spaced longitudinal ribs. Another example, Calamites *cisti*, has much smaller nodes and the ribs are typically closer together.

In addition, the distance between successive node lines on a Calamites suckowi specimen is typically much wider than the diameter. In other forms like Calamites *cisti*, the opposite is true or the specimen is just slightly wider than the diameter.

However, the value of these form taxa is limited. The distance between nodes, for example, is highly variable, and an intercalary meristem means that this distance varied as the organisms grew.

The genus Calamites has been placed in the plant division Equisetophyta (formerly known as Sphenophyta) and family

Calamitaceae. They finally became extinct in the Lower Permian, a time which, however, also saw the origin of the family Equisetaceae, to which the only living sphenophyte genus Equisetum belongs.

CYCAD

Cycads are a group of seed plants characterized by a large crown of compound leaves and a stout trunk. They are evergreen, gymnospermous, dioecious plants having large pinnately compound leaves. They are frequently confused with and mistaken for palms or ferns, but are related to neither, belonging to the division Cycadophyta.

Cycads are found across much of the subtropical and tropical parts of the world. They are found in South and Central America (where the greatest diversity occurs), Mexico, the Antilles, south-eastern United States of America, Australia, Melanesia, Micronesia, Japan, China, Southeast Asia, India, Sri Lanka, Madagascar, and southern and tropical Africa, where at least 65 species occur. Some are renowned for survival in harsh semi-desert climates, and can grow in sand or even on rock. They are able to grow in full sun or shade, and some are salt tolerant. Though they are a minor component of the plant kingdom today, during the Jurassic period they were extremely common.

They have very specialized pollinators and have been reported to fix nitrogen in association with a cyanobacterium living in the roots. This blue-green algae produces a neurotoxin called BMAA that is found in the seeds of cycads.

Origins

There is controversy over older cycad fossils that date to the late Carboniferous period, 300–325 mya. One of the first colonizers of terrestrial habitats, this clade probably diversified extensively within its first few million years, although the extent to which it radiated is unknown because relatively few fossil specimens have been found. The regions to which cycads are restricted probably indicate their former distribution on the supercontinents Laurasia and Gondwana.

The family Stangeriaceae (named for Dr. William Stanger, 1812(?)–1854), consisting of only three extant species, is thought to be of Gondwanan origin as fossils have been found in Lower Cretaceous deposits in Argentina, dating to 70–135 mya. Zamiaceae is more diverse, with a fossil record extending from the Middle Triassic to the Eocene (54–200 mya) in North and South America, Europe, Australia, and Antarctica, implying that the family was present before the break-up of Pangea. Cycadaceae is thought to be an early offshoot from other cycads, with fossils from Eocene deposits (38–54 mya) in Japan and China, indicating that this family originated in Laurasia. Cycas is the only genus in the family and contains 99 species, the most of any cycad genus. Molecular data has recently shown that Cycas species in Australasia and the east coast of Africa are recent arrivals, suggesting that adaptive radiation may have occurred. The current distribution of cycads may be due to radiations from a few ancestral types sequestered on Laurasia and Gondwana, or could be explained by genetic drift following the separation of already evolved genera. Both explanations account for the strict endemism across present continental lines.

Taxonomy

There are about 305 described species, in 10–12 genera and 2–3 families of cycads (depending on taxonomic viewpoint). The classification below, proposed by Dennis Stevenson in 1990, is based upon a hierarchical structure based on cladistic analyses of morphological, anatomical, karyological, physiological and phytochemical data.

The number of species in the clade is low compared to the number of species in most other plant phyla. However, paleobotanical and molecular research indicates that diversity was higher in the history of the phylum. Fossil evidence shows that structural diversity in Mesozoic cycad pollen "considerably exceeds that seen in surviving genera today". The impacts of extinction on diversity are highlighted below. The disparity in molecular sequences is very high between the three main lineages of cycads, implying that genetic diversity in the clade was once high, but this fact has led to major disagreements about the divisions within the Cycadales.

The number of described cycad species has doubled in the past 25 years, mostly due to improved sampling and further exploration. Experts assume there may still be about 100 undescribed species, based on the rate of discovery. These are likely to be in Asia and South America where areas of endemism are highest. Diversity hotspots also occur in Australia, South Africa, Mexico, China and Vietnam, which together account for more than 70% of the world's cycad species. The taxonomy of the Cycadophyta is, however, now stabilizing.

Cycad systematists reject the biological species concept, as clearly defined cycad species can interbreed and produce fertile offspring; this character is thus not disproportionately weighted when determining species barriers. The phenetic species concept, which states that a species is defined based on overall similarities with other individuals of the same species combined with a significant gap in variation with other species, is also rejected. Most cycad taxonomists agree on a modified version of the evolutionary species concept, termed the 'morphogeographic' species concept, which recognises the combined effects of geographical isolation and morphological disparity. Thus the presence of large geographical gaps in cycad distribution has greatly affected the way cycads are classified.

Suborder Cycadineae

Family *Cycadaceae*

Subfamily *Cycadoideae*

About 105 species in the Old World from Africa east to southern Japan, Australia and the western Pacific Ocean islands; type: *C. circinalis L.*; see also *C. pruinosa* and *C. revoluta*

Suborder *Zamiineae*

Family *Stangeriaceae*

Subfamily *Stangerioideae*

Stangeria. One species in southern Africa; type: *S. eriopus* (Kunze) Baillon

Subfamily *Bowenioideae*

Bowenia. Two species in Queensland, Australia; type: B. spectabilis Hook. ex Hook. f.

Family *Zamiaceae*

Subfamily *Encephalartoideae*

Tribe Diooeae

Dioon. 13 species in Mexico and Central America; type: *D. edule* Lindley

Tribe *Encephalarteae*

Subtribe Encephalartinae

Encephalartos. About 66 species in southeast Africa; type: *E. friderici-guilielmi* Lehmann, *E. transvenosus* (Modjadji cycad)

Subtribe *Macrozamiinae*

Macrozamia. About 41 species in Australia; type: *M. riedlei* (Fischer ex Gaudichaud) C.A. Gardner

Lepidozamia. Two species in eastern Australia; type: *L. peroffskyana* Regel

Subfamily *Zamioideae*

Tribe Ceratozamieae

Ceratozamia. 26 species in southern Mexico and Central America; type: C. mexicana Brongn.

Tribe Zamieae

Subtribe Microcycadinae

Microcycas. One species in Cuba; type: *M. calocoma* (Miquel) A. DC.

Subtribe *Zamiinae*

Chigua. Two species in Colombia; type: C. restrepoi E. Stevenson.

Zamia. About 65 species in the New World from Georgia, USA south to Bolivia; type: Z. pumila L.; see also Z. furfuracea.

Cycads are most closely related to the extinct Bennettitales, and are also relatively close relatives to the Ginkgoales, as shown in the following phylogeny:

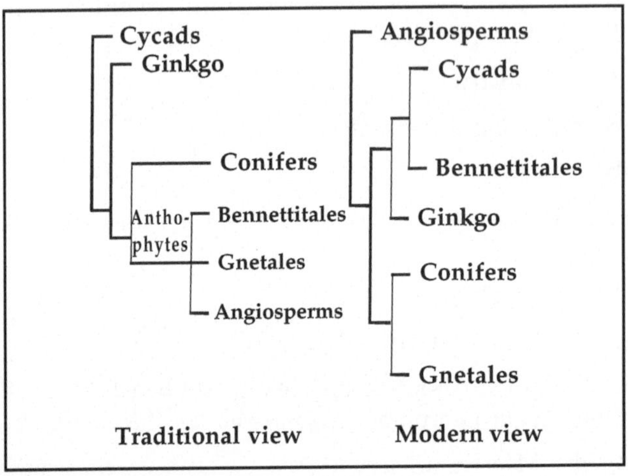

History

Modern knowledge about Cycads began in the 9th century with the recording by two Arab naturalists that the genus Cycas was used as a source of flour in India. Later, in the 16th century, Antonio Pigafetta, Fernao Lopez de Castanheda and Francis Drake found Cycas plants in the Moluccas, where the seeds were eaten. The first report of cycads in the New World was by Giovanni Lerio in his 1576 trip to Brazil, where he observed a plant named ayrius by the indigenous people; this species is now classified in the genus Zamia.

Cycads belonging to the genus *Encephalartos* were first described by Johann Georg Christian Lehmann in 1834. The name is derived from the Greek articles "en", meaning "in", "cephale", meaning "head", and "artos", meaning "bread".

Throughout the 18th-19th centuries, discoveries of several species were reported by numerous naturalist researchers and discoverers traveling throughout the world. One of the most notable researchers of cycads was American botanist C.J. Chamberlain whose work is noteworthy for the quantity of data and the novelty of his approach to studying cycads. His 15 years of travel throughout Africa, the Americas and Australia to observe cycads in their natural habitat resulted in his 1919 publication of *The Living Cycads* which remains current in its synthesis of taxonomy, morphology and reproductive biology of cycads, most of which was obtained from his original research. His 1940s monograph on the Cycadales, though never published (most likely because of his death) was never used by botanists. There are no other complete works on the cycads.

Uses

The generic name refers to the starch obtained from the stems which was used as food by some indigenous tribes. Tribal people grind and soak the nuts to remove the nerve toxin, making the food source generally safe to eat, although often not all the toxin is removed. In addition, consumers of bush meat may face a health threat as the meat comes from game which may have eaten cycad nuts and carry traces of the toxin in body fat.

There is some indication that the regular consumption of starch derived from cycads is a factor in the development of Lytico-Bodig disease, a neurological disease with symptoms similar to those of Parkinson's disease and ALS.

Overall species diversity peaks at 17° 15"N and 28° 12"S, with a minor peak at the equator. There is therefore not a latitudinal diversity gradient towards the equator but towards the tropics. However, the peak in the northern tropics is largely due to Cycas in Asia and Zamia in the New World, whereas the peak in the southern tropics is due to Cycas again, and also to the diverse genus Encephalartos in southern and central Africa and Macrozamia in Australia. Thus the distribution pattern of cycad species with latitude appears to be an artifact of the geographical isolation of cycad genera, and is dependent on the remaining species in each genus that did not follow the extinction pattern of their ancestors. Cycas is the only genus that has a broad geographical range and can thus be used to infer that cycads tend to live in the upper and lower tropics. This is probably because these areas have a drier climate with relatively cool winters; while cycads require some rainfall, they appear to be partly xerophytic. Potted specimens are found and thrive in global locations such as Canada, Russia, Finland, Chile.

Speciation

There are no documented cases of sympatric speciation in cycads and allopatry appears to be the most common form of speciation in the group. This is difficult to study as they are long-lived plants, and so natural experiments have been investigated. One example is *Cycas seemannii*, which occurs only in Fiji, New Caledonia, Tonga and Vanuatu. Genetic diversity within populations was found to be significantly lower than between islands, suggesting that genetic drift is a likely mechanism for speciation, and is probably currently occurring between the isolated populations. Allopatry has also been proposed as the mechanism of speciation in Dioon, which predominantly occurs in Mexico. The many rivers that have shaped the region, and repeated glaciation and consequent disjunction, are thought to have been important in reproductive isolation not only in Dioon but in many other plant and animal taxa. Parapatric speciation may also have occurred, especially as cycads are pollinated by insects rather than by wind. As the range of the species grows, the individuals furthest apart are prevented from interbreeding as insects have relatively small ranges and will not pollinate between these plants. If sympatric speciation has occurred in cycads this would most likely be because of a host shift in pollinators, due to the very fact that cycads are uniformly dioecious.

Extinction

The probable former range of cycads can be inferred from their global distribution. For example, the family Stangeriaceae only contains three extant species, in Africa. Diverse fossils of this family have been dated to 135 mya, indicating that diversity may have been much greater before the Jurassic and late Triassic mass extinction events. However, the cycad fossil record is generally poor and little can be deduced about the effects of each mass extinction event on their diversity.

Instead, correlations can be made between the number of extant gymnosperms and angiosperms. It is likely that cycad diversity was affected more by the great angiosperm radiation in the mid-Cretaceous than by extinctions. Very slow cambial growth was first used to define cycads, and because of this characteristic the group could not compete with the rapidly growing, relatively short-lived angiosperms, which now number over 250,000 species, compared to the 947 remaining gymnosperms. It is surprising that the cycads are still extant, having been faced with extreme competition and five major extinctions. The ability of cycads to survive in relatively dry environments where plant diversity is generally lower, and their great longevity may explain their long persistence.

Conservation

Encephalartos woodii is extinct in the wild, and all living specimens are clones of the typeIn recent years, many cycads have been dwindling in numbers and may face risk of extinction because of theft and unscrupulous collection from their natural habitats, as well as from habitat destruction.

Twenty-three per cent of the 305 extant cycad species are either critically endangered or endangered, and 15% are vulnerable. Thus 38% of cycads are on the IUCN Red List (2004), and the other 62% are in the Least concern or Near Threatened category (i.e. not actually on the Red List), or are data deficient. This value has changed dramatically within the past few years; 46% of cycads were on the 1978 Red List, and this rose to 82% in 1997. This was largely due to the recent discovery of over 150 new species, disagreements about classification, and uncertainty. This has not been helpful for conservation planning for the group.

Zamia in the New World, Cycas in Asia and Encephalartos in Africa are the most threatened genera. This pattern reflects the pressures on species in these regions. At least two species, *Encephalartos woodii* and *Encephalartos relictus* (both from Africa), are confirmed extinct in the wild. Cycads are long-lived with infrequent reproduction, and most populations are small, putting them at risk of extinction from habitat destruction and stochastic environmental events. Regionally, Australian cycads are the least at risk, as they are locally common and habitat fragmentation is low. However, land management with fire is thought to be a threat to Australian species. African cycads are rare and are thought to be naturally decreasing due to small population sizes, and there is controversy over whether to let natural extinction processes act on these cycads.

Horticulture

Cycads can be cut up into pieces to make new plants, although the most environmentally responsible method is by direct planting of the seeds. Propagation by seeds is the preferred method of growth, and two unique risks to their germination exist. One is that the seeds have no dormancy, so that the embryo is biologically required to maintain growth and development, which means if the seed dries out, it dies. The second is that the emerging radicle and embryo can be very susceptible to fungal diseases in its early stages when in unhygienic or excessively wet conditions. Thus, many cycad growers pre-germinate the seeds in moist, sterile media such as vermiculite or perlite. However pre-germination is not necessary, and many report success by directly planting the seeds in regular potting soil. As with many plants, a combination of well-drained soil, sunlight, water and nutrients will help it to prosper. Although, because of their hardy nature, cycads do not necessarily require the most tender or careful treatment, they can grow in almost any medium, including soil-less ones. One of the most common cause of cycad death is from rotting stems and roots due to over-watering.

Some insects, particularly scale insects, some weevils and chewing insects can damage cycads, though the pests are susceptible to insecticides such as the horticulture soluble oil white oil. Sometimes bacterial preparations may be used to control insect infestation on cycads. However, when some of the mature plants prepare for reproduction, the presence of weevils have been shown to help accomplish pollination.

While the cycads have a reputation of slow growth, it is not always well-founded and some actually grow quite fast, achieving reproductive maturity in 2–3 years (as with some Zamia species), while others in 15 years (as with some Cycas, Australian Macrozamia and Lepidozamia).

GLOSSOPTERIS

Glossopteris (Greek glossa, meaning "tongue", because the leaves were tongue-shaped) is the largest and best-known genus of the extinct order of seed ferns known as Glossopteridales (or in some cases as Arberiales or Dictyopteridiales).

History

The Glossopteridales arose around the beginning of the Permian on the great southern continent of Gondwana. These plants went on to become the dominant elements of the southern flora through the rest of the Permian but disappeared in almost all places at the end of the Permian. The only convincing Triassic records are very earliest Triassic leaves from Nidpur in India, but even these records are somewhat questionable owing to faulting and complex juxtapositioning of Permian and Triassic strata at Nidpur. Although most modern palaeobotany textbooks cite the continuation of glossopterids into later parts of the Triassic and, in some cases into the Jurassic, these ranges are erroneous and are based on misidentification of morphologically similar leaves such as Gontriglossa, Sagenopteris, or Mexiglossa. Glossopterids were, therefore, one of the major casualties of the end-Permian mass-extinction event.

More than 70 fossil species of this genus have been recognized in India alone, with additional species from South America, Australia, Africa, Madagascar and Antarctica. Essentially, Glossopteris was restricted to the middle and high latitude parts of Gondwana during the Permian. Most northern parts of South America and Africa lack Glossopteris and its associated organs. However, in recent years a few disparate localities in Morocco, Oman, Anatolia, the western part of the island of New Guinea and Thailand have yielded fossils that are of possible glossopterid affinity. These peri-gondwanan records commonly occur together with Cathaysian or Euramerican plant species - the assemblages representing a zone of mixing between the strongly provincial floras of the Permian. Apart from those in India and the perigondwanan localities, a few other fossils from the Northern Hemisphere have been assigned to this group, but these are not identified with great certainty. For example, specimens assigned to Glossopteris from the far east of Russia in the 1960s are more likely to be misdentifications of other gymnosperms such as Pursongia. Confident assignment of fossil leaves to Glossopteris normally requires their co-preservation with the distinctive segmented roots of this group (called Vertebraria) or with the distinctive fertile organs.

Taxonomy

Long considered a fern after its discovery in 1824, it was later assigned to the gymnosperms. The genus is placed in the division Pteridospermatophyta. In reality, many of the plant groups included within this division are only distantly related to one another. Glossopterids' relationships with other groups remain obscure. Most recent phylogenetic analyses favour placement of glossopterids as sister to a large group including Corystospermales, Caytoniales, Bennettitales, Pentoxylales, Gnetales (in some analyses), and angiosperms. A few analyses favour alternative links with Ginkgoales, Cordaitales and Pinales.

Glossopteris should strictly be used to refer to the distinctive spathulate fossil leaves with reticulate venation, however, the term has also been used to refer to the parent plant as a whole.

The relationship of stem groups to the angiosperms is of utmost importance in determining the evolution of flowers; stem groups provide an insight into the state of earlier "forks" on the path to the current state. If we identify an unrelated group as a stem group, then we will gain an incorrect image of the lineages' history. The traditional view that flowers arose by modification of a structure similar to that of the gnetales, for example, no longer bears weight in the light of the molecular data.

Convergence increases our chances of misidentifying stem groups. Since the protection of the megagametophyte is evolutionarily desirable, it would be unsurprising if many separate groups stumbled upon protective encasements independently. Distinguishing ancestry in such a situation, especially where we usually only have fossils to go on, is tricky – to say the least.

In flowers, this protection is offered by the carpel, an organ believed to represent an adapted leaf, recruited into a protective role, shielding the ovules. These ovules are further protected by a double-walled integument.

Penetration of these protective layers needs something more that a free-floating microgametophyte. Angiosperms have pollen grains comprising just three cells. One cell is responsible for drilling down through the integuments, and creating a conduit for the two sperm cells to flow down. The megagametophyte has just seven cells; of these, one fuses with a sperm cell, forming the nucleus of the egg itself, and another other joins with the other sperm, and dedicates itself to forming a nutrient-rich endosperm. The other cells take auxiliary roles. This process of "double fertilisation" is unique and common to all angiosperms.

Biology

Glossopteris was a woody, seed-bearing shrub or tree, some apparently reaching 30 m tall. They had a softwood interior that resembles conifers of the family Araucariaceae. Seeds and pollen-containing organs were borne in clusters at the tips of slender stalks partially fused (adnate) to the leaves. The homologies of the flattened seed-bearing structures have remained particularly controversial with some arguing that the fertile organs represent megasporophylls (fertile leaves) whereas others have interpreted the structures as flattened, seed-bearing, axillary axes (cladodes).

They are interpreted to have grown in very wet soil conditions, similar to the modern Bald Cypress. The leaves ranged from about 2 cm to over 30 cm in length.

The profile of glossopterid trees is largely speculative as complete trees have not been preserved. However, based on analogies with modern high-latitude plants Glossopteris trees probably tapered upwards like a Christmas tree and were relatively widely spaced to take advantage of the low-angle sunlight at high latitudes. Instead of needles, they had large, broad lance- or tongue-shaped leaves that fell to the ground at the end of summer. The fossil leaves are commonly found as dense accumulations representing autumnal leaf banks. The fossilized tree rings in the Glossopteris trees reveal that they grew steadily each spring-summer and abruptly stopped for winter.

Glossopteris leaves are morphologically simple so there are few characters that can be used to differentiate species. Consequently, many past researchers have considered the Permian Glossopteris flora to be rather homogeneous with the same species distributed throughout the Southern Hemisphere. However, more recent studies of the more morphologically diverse fertile organs have shown that taxa had limited regional distributions and several intra-gondwanan floristic provinces are recognizable. Nevertheless, several species of leaves found in Antarctica are common in the rocks of similar geologic age in India, located north of the equator and half a world away. Seeds, much too large to be wind-borne, could not have blown across thousands of miles of open sea, nor is it likely they have floated across vast oceans. Observations such as these led the Austrian geologist Eduard Suess to deduce that there had once been a land bridge between these areas. He named this large land mass Gondwanaland (named after the district in India where the plant Glossopteris was found). These same observations would also lend support to Alfred Wegener's Continental drift theory.

Rescences of the Bennettitales are Strikingly Similar to Flowers

In the fossil record, there are three intriguing groups which bore flower-like structures. The first is the Permian pteridosperm *Glossopteris,* which already bore recurved leaves resembling carpels. The Triassic *Caytonia* is more flower-like still, with enclosed ovules – but only a single integument. Further, details of their pollen and stamens set them apart from true flowering plants.

The Bennettitales bore remarkably flower-like organs, protected by whorls of bracts which may have played a similar role to the petals and sepals of true flowers; however, these flower-like structures evolved independently, as the Bennettitales are more closely related to cycads and ginkgos than to the angiosperms

However, no true flowers are found in any groups save those extant today. Most morphological and molecular analyses place *Amborella,* the nymphaeales and Austrobaileyaceae in a basal clade dubbed "ANA". This clade appear to have diverged in the early Cretaceous, around 130 million years ago – around the same time as the earliest fossil angiosperm, and just after the first angiosperm-like pollen, 136 million years ago The magnoliids diverged soon after, and a rapid radiation had produced eudicots and monocots by 125 million years ago By the end of the

Cretaceous 65.5 million years ago, over 50% of today's angiosperm orders had evolved, and the clade accounted for 70% of global species.

The features of the basal "ANA" groups suggest that angiosperms originated in dark, damp, frequently disturbed areas It appears that the angiosperms remained constrained to such habitats throughout the Cretaceous – occupying the niche of small herbs early in the successional series This may have restricted their initial significance, but given them the flexibility that accounted for the rapidity of their later diversifications in other habitats.

Advances in Metabolism

The most recent major innovation by the plants is the development of the C_4 metabolic pathway.

Photosynthesis is not quite as simple as adding water to CO_2 to produce sugars and oxygen. A complex chemical pathway is involved in this miraculous reaction, facilitated along the way by a range of enzymes and co-enzymes. The enzyme RuBisCO is responsible for "fixing" CO_2 – that is, it attaches it to a carbon-based molecule to form a sugar, which can be used by the plant, releasing an oxygen molecule along the way. However, the enzyme is notoriously inefficient, and works just as effectively in the other direction through a process known as photorespiration. As well as a hot-off-the press sugar molecule, this also costs the plant energy required to "re-set" the RuBisCO molecule.

Concentrating Carbon

To work around this inefficiency, C_4 plants developed "carbon concentrating" mechanisms. These work by bombarding RuBisCO molecules with CO_2, thereby increasing the amount of time they are performing the useful task of making sugars. The process of bombarding the RuBisCO requires more energy than allowing gasses to come and go where they please, but under the right conditions – i.e. warm temperatures, low CO_2 concentrations, or high oxygen concentrations – pays off in terms of the decreased loss of sugar through photorespiration.

One, C_4 metabolism, employs a so-called Kranz anatomy. This transports CO_2 through an outer mesophyll layer, via a range of organic molecules, to a central bundle sheath cell, where, the CO_2 is released. In this way, CO_2 is concentrated near the site of RuBisCO operation. Because RuBisCO is operating in an environment with much more CO_2 (and less oxygen) than it otherwise would be, it performs more efficiently.

A second method, CAM photosynthesis, temporally separates photosynthesis from the action of RuBisCO. RuBisCO only operates during the day, when stomata are sealed and CO_2 is provided by the breakdown of the chemical malate. More CO_2 is then harvested from the atmosphere when stomata open, during the cool, moist nights, reducing water loss.

Evolutionary Record

These two pathways, with the same effect on RuBisCO, evolved a number of times independently – indeed, C_4 alone arose 18 times! The C_4 construction is most famously used by a subset of grasses, while CAM is employed by many succulents and cacti. The trait appears to have emerged during the Oligocene, around 25 to 32 million years ago however, they did not become ecologically significant until the Miocene, 6-7 million years ago. Remarkably, some charcoalified fossils preserve tissue organised into the Kranz anatomy, with intact bundle sheath cells allowing the presence C_4 metabolism to be identified without doubt at this time. In deducing their distribution and significance, we resort to the use of isotopic markers. C_3 plants preferentially use the lighter of two isotopes of carbon in the atmosphere, ^{12}C, which is more readily involved in the chemical pathways involved in its fixation. Because C_4 metabolism involves a further chemical step, this effect is accentuated. Plant material can be analysed to deduce the ratio of the heavier ^{13}C to ^{12}C. This ratio is denoted $d^{13}C$. C_3 plants are on average around 12% (parts per thousand) lighter than the atmospheric ratio, while C_4 plants are about 27% lighter.

It's troublesome procuring original fossil material in sufficient quantity to analyse the grass itself, but fortunately we have a good proxy: horses. Horses were globally widespread in the period of interest, and browsed almost exclusively on grasses. There's an old phrase in isotope palæontology, "you are what you eat (plus a little bit)" – this refers to the fact that organisms reflect the isotopic composition of whatever they eat, plus a small adjustment factor. There is a good record of horse teeth throughout the globe, and their d[13]C has been measured. The record shows a sharp negative inflection around 6-7 million years ago, during the Messinian, and this is interpreted as the rise of C_4 plants on a global scale.

When is C_4 an Advantage?

While C_4 enhances the efficiency of RuBisCO, the concentration of carbon is highly energy intensive. This means that C_4 plants only have an advantage over C_3 organisms in certain conditions: namely, high temperatures, low CO_2 and high oxygen concentrations. C_4 plants also need high levels of sunlight in order to thrive. Models suggest that without wildfires removing shade-casting trees and shrubs, there would be no space for C_4 plants. But wildfires have occurred for 400 million years – why did C_4 take so long to arise, and then appear independently so many times? The Carboniferous period (~300 million years ago) had notoriously high oxygen levels – almost enough to allow spontaneous combustion – and very low CO_2, but there is no C_4 isotopic signature to be found. And there doesn't seem to be a sudden trigger for the Miocene rise.

During the Micoene, the atmosphere and climate was relatively stable. If anything, it increased gradually from 14 to 9 million years ago before settling down to concentrations similar to the Holocene This suggests that it did not have a key role in invoking C_4 evolution. Grasses themselves (the group which would give rise to the most occurrences of C_4) had probably been around for 60 million years or more, so had had plenty of time to evolve C_4 which in any case is present in a diverse range of groups and thus evolved independently. There is a strong signal of climate change in South Asia increasing aridity – hence increasing fire frequency and intensity – may have led to an increase in the importance of grasslands. However, this is difficult to reconcile with the North American record is possible that the signal is entirely biological, forced by the fire- (and elephant?) driven acceleration of grass evolution – which, both by increasing weathering and incorporating more carbon into sediments, reduced atmospheric CO_2 levels. Finally, there is evidence that the onset of C_4 from 9 to 7 million years ago is a biased signal, which only holds true for North America, from where most samples originate; emerging evidence suggests that grasslands evolved to a dominant state at least 15Ma earlier in South America.

Evolutionary Trends

The process of evolution works slightly differently in plants than animals. Differences in plant physiology and reproduction mean that while the same evolutionary principles of natural selection apply, the finer nuances of their effect are radically different.

One major difference is the ability of plants to reproduce clonally, and the totipotent nature of their cells, allowing them to reproduce asexually much more easily than most animals. They are also capable of polyploidy – where more than two chromosome sets are inherited from parents. This allows relatively fast bursts of evolution to occur. The long periods of dormancy that seed plants can employ also makes them less vulnerable to extinction, as they can "sit out" the tough periods and wait until more clement times to leap back to life.

The effect of these differences is most profoundly seen during extinction events. These events, which wiped out between 6 and 62% of terrestrial animal families, had "negligible" effect on plant families. However, the ecosystem structure is significantly rearranged, with the abundances and distributions of different groups of plants changing profoundly. These effects are perhaps due to the higher diversity within families, as extinction – which *was* common at the species level – was very selective. For example, wind-pollinated species survived better than insect-pollinated taxa, and specialised species generally lost out. In general, the surviving taxa were rare before the extinction, suggesting that they were generalists who were poor competitors when times were easy, but prospered when specialised groups went extinct and left ecological niches vacant.

The relationship of stem groups to the angiosperms is of utmost importance in determining the evolution of flowers; stem groups provide an insight into the state of earlier "forks" on the path to the current state. If we identify an unrelated group as a stem group, then we will gain an incorrect image of the lineages' history. The traditional view that flowers arose by modification of a structure similar to that of the gnetales, for example, no longer bears weight in the light of the molecular data. Convergence increases our chances of misidentifying stem groups. Since the protection of the megagametophyte is evolutionarily desirable, it would be unsurprising if many separate groups stumbled upon protective encasements independently. Distinguishing ancestry in such a situation, especially where we usually only have fossils to go on, is tricky – to say the least.

In flowers, this protection is offered by the carpel, an organ believed to represent an adapted leaf, recruited into a protective role, shielding the ovules. These ovules are further protected by a double-walled integument. Penetration of these protective layers needs something more that a free-floating microgametophyte. Angiosperms have pollen grains comprising just three cells. One cell is responsible for drilling down through the integuments, and creating a conduit for the two sperm cells to flow down. The megagametophyte has just seven cells; of these, one fuses with a sperm cell, forming the nucleus of the egg itself, and another other joins with the other sperm, and dedicates itself to forming a nutrient-rich endosperm. The other cells take auxiliary roles. This process of "double fertilisation" is unique and common to all angiosperms.

EQUISETUM

Equisetum is the only living genus in the Equisetaceae, a family of vascular plants that reproduce by spores rather than seeds. They are commonly known as horsetails.

In fact, Equisetum is the only surviving genus of the entire class Equisetopsida, which for over one hundred million years was very diverse and dominated the understory of late Paleozoic forests. Some Equisetopsida were large trees reaching to 30 m tall; the genus Calamites of family Calamitaceae for example is abundant in coal deposits from the Carboniferous period.

A superficially similar but entirely unrelated flowering plant genus, mare's tail (Hippuris), is occasionally misidentified and misnamed as "horsetail".

Etymology

The name "horsetail", often used for the entire group, arose because the branched species somewhat resemble a horse's tail. Similarly, the scientific name Equisetum derives from the Latin equus ("horse") + seta ("bristle").

Other names include candock for branching individuals, and scouring-rush for unbranched or sparsely branched individuals. The latter name refers to the plants' rush-like appearance, and to the fact that the stems are coated with abrasive silicates, making them useful for scouring (cleaning) metal items such as cooking pots or drinking mugs, particularly those made of tin. In German, the corresponding name is Zinnkraut ("tin-herb"). Rough Horsetail E. hyemale is still boiled and then dried in Japan, to be used for the final polishing process on woodcraft to produce a smoother finish than any sandpaper.

Distribution and Ecology

The genus Equisetum is near-cosmopolitan, being absent only from Australasia and Antarctica. They are perennial plants, either herbaceous and dying back in winter as most temperate species, or evergreen as most tropical species and the temperate species Rough Horsetail (*E. hyemale*), Branched Horsetail (*E. ramosissimum*), Dwarf Horsetail (*E. scirpoides*) and Variegated Horsetail (*E. variegatum*). They mostly grow 0.2-1.5 m tall, though the "giant horsetail" are recorded to grow as high as 2.5 m (Northern Giant Horsetail, *E. telmateia*), 5 m (Southern Giant Horsetail, *E. giganteum*) or 8 m (Mexican Giant Horsetail, *E. myriochaetum*), and allegedly even more.

Many plants in this genus prefer wet sandy soils, though some are semi-aquatic and others are adapted to wet clay soils. The stalks arise from rhizomes that are deep underground and almost impossible to dig out. The Field Horsetail (E. arvense) can be a nuisance weed, readily regrowing from the rhizome after being pulled out. It is also unaffected by many herbicides designed to kill seed plants.

If eaten in large quantities, the foliage of some species is poisonous to grazing animals, including (somewhat ironically given its common name) horses. On the other hand some species are cooked and eaten by humans in Japan.

Anatomy

In these plants the leaves are greatly reduced and usually non-photosynthetic. They contain a single, non-branching vascular trace, which is the defining feature of microphylls. However, it has recently been recognised that horsetail microphylls are probably not primitive like in Lycopodiophyta (clubmosses and relatives), but rather advanced adaptations, evolved by the reduction of a megaphyll. They are therefore sometimes actually referred to as megaphylls to reflect this homology.

The leaves of horsetails grow in whorls fused into nodal sheaths. The stems are green and photosynthetic, and distinctive in being hollow, jointed and ridged (with sometimes 3 but usually 6-40 ridges). There may or may not be whorls of branches at the nodes; when present, these branches are identical to the main stem except being smaller and more delicate.

Spores

The spores are borne under sporangiophores in strobili, cone-like structures at the tips of some of the stems. In many species the cone-bearing stems are unbranched, and in some (e.g. Field Horsetail, *E. arvense*) they are non-photosynthetic, produced early in spring separately from photosynthetic sterile stems. In some other species (e.g. Marsh Horsetail, *E. palustre*) they are very similar to sterile stems, photosynthetic and with whorls of branches.

Horsetails are mostly homosporous, though in the Field Horsetail smaller spores give rise to male prothalli. The spores have four elaters that act as moisture-sensitive springs, assisting spore dispersal after the sporangia have split open longitudinally.

Evolution and Systematics

The Equisetopsida were formerly regarded as a separate division of spore plants and also called Arthrophyta or

Sphenophyta; today they have been recognized as rather close relatives of the typical ferns (Pteridopsida) and form a specialized lineage of the Pteridophyta.

As mentioned above, all living horsetails are placed in the genus Equisetum. But there are some fossil species that are not assignable to the modern genus:

Pseudobornia contains the oldest known Equisetaceae it grew in the late Devonian, about 375 million years ago.

Equisetites is a "wastebin taxon" uniting all sorts of large horsetails from the Mesozoic; it is almost certainly paraphyletic and would probably warrant to be subsumed in Equisetum. But while some of the species placed there are likely to be ancestral to the modern horsetails, there have been reports of secondary growth in other Equisetites, and these probably represent a distinct and now-extinct horsetail lineage. Equicalastrobus is the name given to fossil horsetail strobili, which probably mostly or completely belong to the (sterile) plants placed in Equisetites.

Species

The living members of the genus Equisetum are divided into two distinct lineages, which are treated as subgenera. Hybridogenic species are common, but such hybridization has only been recorded between members of the same subgenus.

In addition, there are numerous ill-determined populations. One of them, the Kamchatka Horsetail ("Equisetum camtschatcense", is an ornamental forming imposing stands of these archaic plants.

Subgenus Equisetum

Equisetum arvense – Field Horsetail, Common Horsetail

Equisetum bogotense – Andean Horsetail

Equisetum diffusum – Himalayan Horsetail

Equisetum fluviatile – Water Horsetail

Equisetum palustre – Marsh Horsetail

Equisetum pratense – Meadow Horsetail, Shade Horsetail, Shady Horsetail

Equisetum sylvaticum – Wood Horsetail

Equisetum telmateia – Great Horsetail, Northern Giant Horsetail, "giant horsetail"

Branched Horsetail (E. ramosissimum)Subgenus Hippochaete

Equisetum giganteum – Southern Giant Horsetail, "giant horsetail"

Equisetum myriochaetum Schlecht. & Cham. – Mexican Giant Horsetail, "giant horsetail"

Equisetum hyemale – Rough Horsetail, Scouringrush Horsetail

Equisetum laevigatum – Smooth Horsetail

Equisetum ramosissimum Desf. – Branched Horsetail

Equisetum scirpoides Michx. – Dwarf Horsetail

Equisetum variegatum – Variegated Horsetail

Named hybrids

Equisetum × moorei (Rough Horsetail × Branched Horsetail)Hybrids between species in subgenus Equisetum

Equisetum × bowmanii C.N.Page (*Equisetum sylvaticum* × *Equisetum telmateia*)

Equisetum × dycei C.N.Page (*Equisetum fluviatile* × *Equisetum palustre*)

Equisetum × font-queri Rothm. (*Equisetum palustre* × *Equisetum telmateia*)

Equisetum × litorale Kühlew ex Rupr. (*Equisetum arvense* × *Equisetum fluviatile*)

Equisetum × mildeanum Rothm. (*Equisetum pratense* × *Equisetum sylvaticum*)

Equisetum × robertsii Dines (*Equisetum arvense* × *Equisetum telmateia*)

Equisetum × rothmaleri C.N.Page (*Equisetum arvense* × *Equisetum palustre*)

Equisetum × willmotii C.N.Page (*Equisetum fluviatile* × *Equisetum telmateia*)

Hybrids between species in subgenus Hippochaete

Equisetum × ferrissii Clute (*Equisetum hyemale* × *Equisetum laevigatum*)

Equisetum × moorei Newman (*Equisetum hyemale* × *Equisetum ramosissimum*)

Equisetum × nelsonii (A.A.Eat.) Schaffn. (*Equisetum laevigatum* × *Equisetum variegatum*)

Equisetum × schaffneri Milde (*Equisetum giganteum* × *Equisetum myriochaetum*)

Equisetum × trachydon A.Braun (*Equisetum hyemale* × *Equisetum variegatum*)

13

Timeline of Plant Evolution

INTRODUCTION

Plant evolution is an aspect of the study of biological evolution, involving predominantly the evolution of plants suited to live on land, the greening of the various land masses by the filling of their niches with land plants, and the diversification of the groups of land plants

Earliest Classifiable Plants

In the strictly modern sense, the name plant refers to the biological classification kingdom Plantae. However, other photosynthetic organisms, including protists, green algae, and cyanobacteria have evolutionary significance to modern plants. While this article is directly about the evolutionary history of the Plant kingdom, these other organisms provide clues to the evolution of all photosynthetic organisms. All of these organisms, plants, green algae, and the protists, are primary photosynthetic eukaryotic organisms.

Scientists start the search for fossil evidence of plants with indirect evidence for their presence, the evidence of photosynthesis in the geological record. The evidence for photosynthesis in the rock record is varied, but primary evidence comes from around 3000 Ma, in rock records and fossil evidence of cyanobacteria, a photosynthesizing prokaryotic organism. Cyanobacteria use water as a reducing agent, thereby producing atmospheric oxygen as a waste product, and profoundly changing the early reducing atmosphere of the earth to one in which modern aerobic organisms eventually evolved. This oxygen liberated by the cyanobacteria then oxidized dissolved iron in the oceans, the iron precipitated out of the sea water, and fell to the ocean floor to form sedimentary layers of oxidized iron called Banded Iron Formations (BIFs). These BIFs are part of the geological record of evidence for the evolutionary history of plants by identifying when photosynthesis originated. This also provides deep time constraints upon when enough oxygen could have been available in the atmosphere to create the ultraviolet blocking stratospheric ozone layer. The oxygen concentration in the ancient atmosphere subsequently rose, acting as a poison for anaerobic organism, and creating a highly oxidizing atmosphere with niches on land for aerobic organisms.

Evidence for the cyanobacteria also comes from the presence of stromatolites in the fossil record deep into the Precambrian. Stromatolites are layered structures thought to have been formed by the trapping, binding, and cementation of sedimentary grains by microorganisms, such as cyanobacteria. The direct evidence for cyanobacteria is less certain than the evidence for their presence as primary producers of atmospheric oxygen.

Chloroplasts in eukaryotic plants evolved from an endosymbiotic relationship between cyanobacteria and another prokaryotic organism, creating a the lineage that eventually led to photosynthesizing eukaryotic organisms in marine and freshwater environments. These earliest photosynthesizing single-celled plants eventually evolved to an organism such as the Charophyta, fresh-water green algae.

CAMBRIAN FLORA

Early plants were small, unicellular or filamentous, composed mostly of soft body tissues, with simple branching. The identification of plant tissues in Cambrian strata is an uncertain area in the evolutionary history of plants because of the small and soft-bodied nature of these plants. It is also difficult in a fossil of this age to distinguish among various similar appearing groups with simple branching patterns, and not all of these groups are plants. One exception to the uncertainty of fossils from this age is the calcareous green algae, Dasycladales found in the fossil record since the middle Cambrian. This algae does not belong to the lineage that is ancestral to the land plants. Other major groups of green algae had been established by this time. Generally, it is accepted that there were no land plants with vascular tissues at this time although some Biologists believe that the molecular clock points to an earlier Cambrian or perhaps Precambrian origin because the molecular clock states that land plants appeared around 480-440 mya and fungi appeared on land around 1 Bya but however there is debate over whether the fossil evidence supports this interpretation of the molecular clock.

ORDOVICIAN FLORA

The evidence for plant evolutionary history changes dramatically in the Ordovician with the first extensive appearance of spores in the fossil record (Cambrian spores have been found, also). The first terrestrial plants appeared in the form of tiny plants resembling liverworts when, around the Middle Ordovician, evidence for the beginning of the terrestrialization of the land is found. These early plants did not have conducting tissues, severely limiting their size. They were, in effect, tied to wet terrestrial environments by their inability to conduct water, like extant liverworts, hornworts, and mosses, although they reproduced with spores, important dispersal units that have hard protective outer coatings, allowing for their preservation in the fossil record, in addition to protecting the future offspring against the desiccating environment of life on land. With spores, plants on land could sent out large numbers of spores that could grow into an adult plant when sufficient environmental moisture was present.

SILURIAN FLORA

Artist's impression of Cooksonia the first fossil records of vascular plants, that is, land plants with vascular tissues, appeared in the Silurian period. The earliest known representatives of this group are Cooksonia (mostly from the northern hemisphere) and Baragwanathia (from Australia). A primitive Silurian land plant with xylem and phloem but no differentiation in root, stem or leaf, was much-branched Psilophyton, reproducing by spores and breathing through stomata on every surface, and probably photosynthesizing in every tissue exposed to light. Rhyniophyta and primitive lycopods were other land plants that first appear during this period.

DEVONIAN FLORA

By the Devonian Period, life was well underway in its colonization of the land. The bacterial and algal mats were joined early in the period by primitive plants that created the first recognizable soils and harbored some arthropods like mites, scorpions and myriapods. Early Devonian plants did not have roots or leaves like the plants most common today, and many had no vascular tissue at all. They probably spread largely by vegetative growth, and did not grow much more than a few centimetres tall.

By the Late Devonian, forests of small, primitive plants existed: lycophytes, sphenophytes, ferns, and progymnosperms had evolved. Most of these plants have true roots and leaves, and many were quite tall. The tree-like ancestral fern Archaeopteris and the giant cladoxylopsid trees grew as a large tree with true wood. These are the oldest known trees of the world's first forests. Prototaxites was the fruiting body of an enormous fungus that stood more than 8 meter tall. By the end of the Devonian, the first seed-forming plants had appeared. This rapid appearance of so many plant groups and growth forms has been called the "Devonian Explosion". The primitive arthropods co-evolved with this diversified terrestrial vegetation structure. The evolving co-dependence of insects and seed-plants that characterizes a recognizably modern world had its genesis in the late Devonian. The development of soils and plant root systems probably led to changes in the speed and pattern of erosion and sediment deposition.

The 'greening' of the continents acted as a carbon dioxide sink, and atmospheric levels of this greenhouse gas may have dropped. This may have cooled the climate and led to a massive extinction event. see Late Devonian extinction. Also in the Devonian, both vertebrates and arthropods were solidly established on the land.

CARBONIFEROUS FLORA

Early Carboniferous land plants were very similar to those of the preceding Latest Devonian, but new groups also appeared at this time.

The main Early Carboniferous plants were the Equisetales (Horse-tails), Sphenophyllales (scrambling plants), Lycopodiales (Club mosses), Lepidodendrales (scale trees), Filicales (Ferns), Medullosales (previously included in the "seed ferns", an artificial assemblage of a number of early gymnosperm groups) and the Cordaitales. These continued to dominate throughout the period, but during late Carboniferous, several other groups, Cycadophyta (cycads), the Callistophytales (another group of "seed ferns"), and the Voltziales (related to and sometimes included under the conifers), appeared.

The Carboniferous lycophytes of the order Lepidodendrales, which are cousins (but not ancestors) of the tiny club-moss of today, were huge trees with trunks 30 metres high and up to 1.5 metres in diameter. These included Lepidodendron (with its fruit cone called Lepidostrobus), Halonia, Lepidophloios and Sigillaria. The roots of several of these forms are known as Stigmaria.

The fronds of some Carboniferous ferns are almost identical with those of living species. Probably many species were epiphytic. Fossil ferns and "seed ferns" include Pecopteris, Cyclopteris, Neuropteris, Alethopteris, and Sphenopteris; Megaphyton and Caulopteris were tree ferns.

The Equisetales included the common giant form Calamites, with a trunk diameter of 30 to 60 cm and a height of up to 20 metres. Sphenophyllum was a slender climbing plant with whorls of leaves, which was probably related both to the calamites and the lycopods.

Cordaites, a tall plant (6 to over 30 metres) with strap-like leaves, was related to the cycads and conifers; the catkin-like inflorescence, which bore yew-like berries, is called Cardiocarpus. These plants were thought to live in swamps and mangroves. True coniferous trees (Waichia, of the order Voltziales) appear later in the Carboniferous, and preferred higher drier ground.

PERMIAN FLORA

The Permian began with the Carboniferous flora still flourishing. About the middle of the Permian there was a major transition in vegetation. The swamp-loving lycopod trees of the Carboniferous, such as Lepidodendron and Sigillaria, were replaced by the more advanced conifers, which were better adapted to the changing climatic conditions. Lycopods and swamp forests still dominated the South China continent because it was an isolated continent and it sat near or at the equator. Oxygen levels were probably high there. The Permian saw the radiation of many important conifer groups, including the ancestors of many present-day families. The ginkgos and cycads also appeared during this period. Rich forests were present in many areas, with a diverse mix of plant groups. The gigantopterids thrived during this time; some of these may have been part of the ancestral flowering plant lineage, though flowers evolved only considerably later.

- Mesozoic Flora;
- Triassic Flora; and
- Jurassic Flora.

The arid, continental conditions characteristic of the Triassic steadily eased during the Jurassic period, especially at higher latitudes; the warm, humid climate allowed lush jungles to cover much of the landscape. Conifers dominated the flora, as during the Triassic; they were the most diverse group and constituted the majority of large trees. Extant conifer families that flourished during the Jurassic included the Araucariaceae, Cephalotaxaceae, Pinaceae, Podocarpaceae, Taxaceae and Taxodiaceae. The extinct Mesozoic conifer family Cheirolepidiaceae dominated low latitude vegetation, as did the shrubby Bennettitales. Cycads were also common, as were ginkgos and tree ferns in the forest. Smaller ferns were probably the dominant undergrowth. Caytoniaceous seed ferns were another group of important plants during this time and are thought to have been shrub to small-tree sized Ginkgo-like plants were particularly common in the mid- to high northern latitudes. In the Southern Hemisphere, podocarps were especially successful, while Ginkgos and Czekanowskiales were rare.

CRETACEOUS FLORA

Artist's restoration of Archaeamphora longicervia, the earliest known carnivorous plantFlowering plants, also known as angiosperms, spread during this period, although they did not become predominant until near the end of the period (Campanian age). Their evolution was aided by the appearance of bees; in fact angiosperms and insects are a good example of coevolution. The first representatives of many modern trees, including figs, planes and magnolias, appeared in the Cretaceous. At the same time, some earlier Mesozoic gymnosperms, like Conifers continued to thrive, although other taxa like Bennettitales died out before the end of the period.

CENOZOIC FLORA

The Cenozoic is just as much the age of savannas, or the age of co-dependent flowering plants and insects. At 35 Ma, grasses evolved from among the angiosperms. About ten thousand years ago, humans in the Fertile Crescent of the Middle East develop agriculture. Plant domestication begins with cultivation of Neolithic founder crops. This process of food production, coupled later with the domestication of animals caused a massive increase in human population that has continued to the present. In Jericho (modern Israel), there is a settlement with about 19,000 people. At the same time, Sahara is green with rivers, lakes, cattles, crocodiles and monsoons. At 8 ka, Common (Bread) wheat (*Triticum aestivum*) originates in southwest Asia due to hybridisation of emmer wheat with a goat-grass, Aegilops tauschii. At 6.5 ka, two rice species are domesticated: Asian rice, Oryza sativa, and African rice *Oryza glaberrima.*

- Species Differentiation;
- Development of rooted plants;
- Flowering plants vs. Conifers;
- Ferns and other primitive plants; and
- Borderline species such as coliform protists.

PLANT EVOLUTIONARY DEVELOPMENTAL BIOLOGY

Evolutionary developmental biology (evo-devo) refers to the study of developmental programs and patterns from an evolutionary perspective It seeks to understand the various influences shaping the form and nature of life on the planet. Evo-devo arose as a separate branch of science only in the last decade Most of the synthesis in evo-devo has been in the field of animal evolution, one reason being the presence of elegant model systems like Drosophila, *C. elegans, Zebra fish* and *Xenopus*. However, in the past couple of decades, a wealth of information on plant morphology, coupled with modern molecular techniques has helped shed light on the conserved and unique developmental patterns in the plant kingdom also.

Historical Perspective

The origin of the term "morphology" is generally attributed to Johann Wolfgang von Goethe. He was of the opinion that there is an underlying fundamental organisation (Bauplan) in the diversity of flowering plants. In his book titled The Metamorphosis of Plants, he proposed that the Bauplan enabled us to predict the forms of plants that had not yet been discovered Goethe also was the first to make the perceptive suggestion that flowers consist of modified leaves.

In the middle centuries, several basic foundations of our current understanding of plant morphology were laid down. Nehemiah Grew, Marcello Malpighi, Robert Hooke, Antonie van Leeuwenhoek, Wilhelm von Nageli were just some of the people who helped build knowledge on plant morphology at various levels of organisation. It was the taxonomical classification of *Carolus linnaeus* in the eighteenth century though, that generated a firm base for the knowledge to stand on and expand. The introduction of the concept of Darwinism in contemporary scientific discourse also had had an effect on the thinking on plant forms and their evolution.

Wilhelm Hofmeister, one of the most brilliant botanists of his times, was the one to diverge away from the idealist way of pursuing botany. Over the course of his life, he brought an interdisciplinary outlook into botanical thinking. He came up with biophysical explanations on phenomena like phototaxis and geotaxis, and also discovered the alternation of generations in the plant life cycle.

The past century witnessed a rapid progress in the study of plant anatomy. The focus shifted from the population level to more reductionist levels. While the first half of the century saw expansion in developmental knowledge at the tissue and the organ level, in the latter half, especially since the 1990s, there has also been a strong impetus on gaining molecular information.

Edward Charles Jeffrey was one of the early evo devo researchers of the 20th century. He performed a comparative analyses of the vasculatures of living and fossil Gymnosperms and came to the conclusion that the storage parenchyma has been derived from tracheids His research focussed primarily on plant anatomy in the context of phylogeny. This tradition of evolutionary analyses of plant architectures was further advanced by Katherine Esau, best known for her book *The Plant Anatomy*. Her work focussed on the origin and development of various tissues in different plants. Working with Cheadle, she also explained the evolutionary specialization of the phloem tissue with respect to its function.

In the meantime, by the beginning of the latter half of 1900s, Arabidopsis thaliana had begun to be used in some developmental studies. The first collection of Arabidopsis thaliana mutants were made around 1945. However it formally became established as a model organism only in 1998.

The recent spurt in information on various plant-related processes has largely been a result of the revolution in molecular biology. Powerful techniques like mutagenesis and complementation were made possible in Arabidopsis via generation of T-DNA containing mutant lines, recombinant plasmids, techniques like Transposon Tagging etc. Availability of complete physical and genetic maps, RNAi vectors, rapid transformation protocols are some of the technologies that have significantly altered the scope of the field. Recently, there has also been a massive increase in the genome and EST sequences of various non-model species, which, coupled with the Bioinformatics tools existing today, generate interesting opportunities in the field of plant evo devo research.

Organisms, Databases and Tools

The most important model systems in plant development have been Arabidopsis and Maize. Maize has traditionally been the favorite of plant geneticists, while extensive resources in almost every area of plant physiology and development are available for Arabidopsis. Apart from these, Rice, Antirrhinum, Brassica, Tomato are also being used in a variety of studies. The genomes of Arabidopsis and Rice have been completely sequenced, while the others are in process It must be emphasized here that the information from these "model" organisms form the basis of our developmental knowledge. While Brassica has been used primarily because of its convenient location in the phylogenetic tree in the mustard family, Antirrhinum is a convenient system for studying leaf architecture. Rice has been traditionally used for studying responses to hormones like abscissic acid and gibberelin as well as responses to stress. However, recently, not just the domesticated rice strain, but also the wild strains have been studied for their underlying genetic architectures.

Some people have objected against extending the results of model organisms to the plant world. One argument is that the effect of gene knockouts in lab conditions wouldn't truly reflect even the same plant's response in the natural world. Also, these supposedly crucial genes might not be responsible for the evolutionary origin of that character. For these reasons, a comparative study of plant traits has been proposed as the way to go now.

Since the past few years, researchers have indeed begun looking at non-model, "non-conventional" organisms using modern genetic tools. One example of this is the Floral Genome Project, which envisages to study the evolution of the current patterns in the genetic architecture of the flower through comparative genetic analyses, with a focus on EST sequences Like the FGP, there are several such ongoing projects that aim to find out conserved and diverse patterns in evolution of the plant shape. Expressed sequence tag (EST) sequences of quite a few non-model plants like Sugarcane, Apple, Lotus, Barley, Cycas, Coffee, to name a few, are available freely online The Cycad Genomics Project for example, aims to understand the differences in structure and function of genes between gymnosperms and angiosperms through sampling in the order Cycadales. In the process, it intends to make available information for the study of evolution of structures like seeds, cones and evolution of life cycle patterns. Presently the most important sequenced genomes from an evo-devo point of view include those of A.thaliana (a flowering plant), Poplar (a woody plant), Physcomitrella patens (a bryophyte), Maize (extensive genetic information), and Chlamydomonas reinhardtii (a green alga). The impact of such a vast amount of information on understanding common underlying developmental mechanisms can easily be realised.

Apart from EST and genome sequences, several other tools like PCR, Yeast two hybrid system, microarrays, RNA Interference, SAGE, QTL mapping etc. permit the rapid study of plant developmental patterns. Recently, cross-species hybridization has begun to be employed on microarray chips, to study the conservation and divergence in mRNA expression patterns between closely related species. Techniques for analyzing this kind of data have also progressed over the past decade. We now have better models for molecular evolution, more refined analysis algorithms and better computing power as a result of advances in computer sciences.

EVOLUTION OF PLANT MORPHOLOGY

Evidence suggests that an algal scum formed on the land 1200 million years ago, but it was not until the Ordovician period, around 500 million years ago, that land plants appeared. These begun to diversify in the late Silurian period, around 420 million years ago, and the fruits of their diversification are displayed in remarkable detail in an early Devonian fossil assemblage known as the Rhynie chert. This chert preserved early plants in cellular detail, petrified in volcanic springs. By the middle of the Devonian period most of the features recognised in plants today are present, including roots, leaves and seeds. By the late Devonian, plants had reached a degree of sophistication that allowed them to form forests of tall trees. Evolutionary innovation continued after the Devonian period. Most plant groups were relatively unscathed by the Permo-Triassic extinction event, although the structures of communities changed. This may have set the scene for the evolution of flowering plants in the Triassic (~200 million years ago), which exploded the Cretaceous and Tertiary. The latest major group of plants to evolve were the grasses, which became important in the mid Tertiary, from around 40 million years ago. The grasses, as well as many other groups, evolved new mechanisms of metabolism to survive the low CO2 and warm, dry conditions of the tropics over the last 10 million years.

Evolution of Meristems

The meristematic cells give rise to various organs of the plant, and keep the plant growing. The Shoot Apical Meristem (SAM) gives rise to organs like the leaves and flowers. The cells of the apical meristems - SAM and RAM (Root Apical Meristem)- divide rapidly and are considered to be indeterminate, in that they do not possess any defined end fate. In that sense, the meristematic cells are frequently compared to the stem cells in animals, that have an analogous behavior and function.

Diversity in Meristem Architectures

Is the mechanism of being indeterminate conserved in the SAM's of the plant world? The SAM contains a population of stem cells that also produce the lateral meristems while the stem elongates. It turns out that the mechanism of regulation of the stem cell number might indeed be evolutionarily conserved. The CLAVATA gene CLV2 responsible for maintaining the stem cell population in Arabidopsis is very closely related to the Maize gene FASCIATED EAR 2(FEA2) also involved in the same function. Similarly, in Rice, the FON1-FON2 system seems to bear a close relationship with the CLV signaling system in Arabidopsis These studies suggest that the regulation of stem cell number, identity and differentiation might be an evolutionarily conserved mechanism in monocots, if not in angiosperms. Rice also contains another genetic system distinct from FON1-FON2, that is involved in regulating stem cell number. This example underlines the innovation that goes about in the living world all the time.

Genetics screens have identified genes belonging to the KNOX family in this function. These genes essentially maintain the stem cells in an undifferentiated state. The KNOX family has undergone quite a bit of evolutionary diversification, while keeping the overall mechanism more or less similar. Members of the KNOX family have been found in plants as diverse as Arabidopsis, rice, barley and tomato. KNOX-like genes are also present in some algae, mosses, ferns and gymnosperms. Misexpression of these genes leads to formation of interesting morphological features. For example, among members of Antirrhinae, only the species of genus Antirrhinum lack a structure called spur in the floral region. A spur is considered an evolutionary innovation because it defines pollinator specificity and attraction. Researchers carried out transposon mutagenesis in Antirrhinum, and saw that some insertions led to formation of spurs that were very similar to the other members of Antirrhinae, indicating that the loss of spur in wild Antirrhinum populations could probably be an evolutionary innovation.

The KNOX family has also been implicated in leaf shape evolution. One study looked at the pattern of KNOX gene expression in A.thaliana, that has simple leaves and Cardamine hirsuta, a plant having complex leaves. In A.thaliana, the KNOX genes are completely turned off in leaves, but in *C. hirsuta*, the expression continued, generating complex leaves. Also, it has been proposed that the mechanism of KNOX gene action is conserved across all vascular plants, because there is a tight correlation between KNOX expression and a complex leaf morphology.

Evolution of the Meristem Architecture

The meristem architectures do differ between angiosperms, gymnosperms and pteridophytes. The gymnosperm vegetative meristem lacks organization into distinct tunica and corpus layers. They possess large cells called Central Mother Cells in the meristem. In angiosperms, the outermost layer of cells divides anticlinally to generate the new cells, while in gymnosperms, the plane of division in the meristem differs for different cells. However, the apical cells do contain organelles like large vacuoles and starch grains, like the angiosperm meristematic cells.

Pteridophytes, like fern, on the other hand, do not possess a multicellular apical meristem. They possess a tetrahedral apical cell, which goes on to form the plant body. Any somatic mutation in this cell can lead to hereditary transmission of that mutation. The earliest meristem-like organization is seen in an algal organism from group Charales that has a single dividing cell at the tip, much like the pteridophytes, yet more simpler. One can thus see a clear pattern in evolution of the meristematic tissue, from pteridophytes to angiosperms. Pteridophytes, with a single meristematic cell; gymnosperms with a multicellular, but less defined organization and finally, angiosperms, with the highest degree of organization. The genetic innovations that contributed to this evolution are yet not clearly known.

Evolution of Leaves

Leaves are the primary photosynthetic organs of a plant. Based on their structure, they are classified into two types - microphylls, that lack complex venation patterns and megaphylls, that are large and with a complex venation. It has been proposed that these structures arose independently. Megaphylls, according to the Telome hypothesis, have evolved from plants that showed a three dimensional branching architecture, through three transformations - planation, which involved formation of a planar architecture, webbing, or formation of the outgrowths between the planar branches and fusion, where these webbed outgrowths fused to form a proper leaf lamina. Studies have revealed that these three steps happened multiple times in the evolution of today's leaves.

It has been proposed that the before the evolution of leaves, plants had the photosynthetic apparatus on the stems. Today's megaphyll leaves probably became commonplace some 360mya, about 40my after the simple leafless plants had colonized the land in the early Devonian period. This spread has been linked to the fall in the atmospheric carbon dioxide concentrations in the Late Paleozoic era associated with a rise in density of stomata on leaf surface. This must have allowed for better transpiration rates and gas exchange. Large leaves with less stomata would have gotten heated up in the sun's heat, but an increased stomatal density allowed for a better-cooled leaf, thus making its spread feasible.

Factors Influencing Leaf Architectures

Spiny leaves of *Aciphylla squarrosa*. It is thought that these leaves evolved as an adaptation against the now extinct. Various physical and physiological forces like light intensity, humidity, temperature, wind speeds etc. are thought to have influenced evolution of leaf shape and size. It is observed that high trees rarely have large leaves, owing to the obstruction they generate for winds. This obstruction can eventually lead to the tearing of leaves, if they are large. Similarly, trees that grow in temperate or taiga regions have pointed leaves, presumably to prevent nucleation of ice onto the leaf surface and reduce water loss due to transpiration. Herbivory, not only by large mammals, but also small insects has been implicated as a driving force in leaf evolution, an example being plants of the genus Aciphylla, that are commonly found in New Zealand. The now extinct Moas fed upon these plants, and its seen that the leaves have spines on their bodies, which probably functioned to discourage the moas from feeding on them. Other members of Aciphylla that did not co-exist with the moas, do not have these spines.

Genetic Evidences for Leaf Evolution

At the genetic level, developmental studies have shown that repression of the KNOX genes is required for initiation of the leaf primordium. This is brought about by ARP genes, which encode transcription factors. Genes of this type have been found in many plants studied till now, and the mechanism i.e.

repression of KNOX genes in leaf primordia, seems to be quite conserved. Interestingly, expression of KNOX genes in leaves produces complex leaves. It is speculated that the ARP function arose quite early in vascular plant evolution, because members of the primitive group Lycophytes also have a functionally similar gene. Other players that have a conserved role in defining leaf primordia are the phytohormone auxin, gibberelin and cytokinin.

One interesting feature of a plant is its phyllotaxy. The arrangement of leaves on the plant body is such that the plant can maximally harvest light under the given constraints, and hence, one might expect the trait to be genetically robust. However, it may not be so. In maize, a mutation in only one gene called abphyl (ABNORMAL PHYLLOTAXY) was enough to change the phyllotaxy of the leaves. It implies that sometimes, mutational tweaking of a single locus on the genome is enough to generate diversity. The abphyl gene was later on shown to encode a cytokinin response regulator protein.

Once the leaf primordial cells are established from the SAM cells, the new axes for leaf growth are defined, one important (and more studied) among them being the abaxial-adaxial (lower-upper surface) axes. The genes involved in defining this, and the other axes seem to be more or less conserved among higher plants. Proteins of the HD-ZIPIII family have been implicated in defining the adaxial identity. These proteins deviate some cells in the leaf primordium from the default abaxial state, and make them adaxial. It is believed that in early plants with leaves, the leaves just had one type of surface - the abaxial one. This is the underside of today's leaves. The definition of the adaxial identity occurred some 200 million years after the abaxial identity was established One can thus imagine the early leaves as an intermediate stage in evolution of today's leaves, having just arisen from spiny stem-like outgrowths of their leafless ancestors, covered with stomata all over, and not optimized as much for light harvesting.

How the infinite variety of plant leaves is generated is a subject of intense research. Some common themes have emerged. One of the most significant is the involvement of KNOX genes in generating compound leaves, as in tomato. But this again is not universal. For example, pea uses a different mechanism for doing the same thing Mutations in genes affecting leaf curvature can also change leaf form, by changing the leaf from flat, to a crinky shape like the shape of cabbage leaves. There also exist different morphogen gradients in a developing leaf which define the leaf's axis. Changes in these morphogen gradients may also affect the leaf form. Another very important class of regulators of leaf development are the microRNAs, whose role in this process has just begun to be documented. The coming years should see a rapid development in comparative studies on leaf development, with many EST sequences involved in the process coming online.

Evolution of Flowers

A flower is, arguably, one of the most beautiful products of evolution. Flower-like structures first appear in the fossil records some ~130 mya, in the Cretaceous era.

The flowering plants have long been assumed to have evolved from within the gymnosperms; according to the traditional morphological view, they are closely allied to the gnetales. However, recent molecular evidence is at odds to this hypothesis, and further suggests that gnetales are more closely related to some gymnosperm groups than angiosperms and that gymnosperms form a distinct clade to the angiosperms. Molecular clock analysis predicts the divergence of flowering plants (anthophytes) and gymnosperms to ~300 mya.

The main function of a flower is reproduction, which, before the evolution of the flower and angiosperms, was the job of microsporophylls and megasporophylls. A flower can be considered a powerful evolutionary innovation, because its presence allowed the plant world to access new means and mechanisms for reproduction.

Origins of the Flower

The family Amborellaceae is regarded as the sister family of all living flowering plants. That means members of this family were most likely the first flowering plants.

It seems that on the level of the organ, the leaf may be the ancestor of the flower, or at least some floral organs. When we mutate some crucial genes involved in flower development, we end up with a cluster of leaf-like structures. Thus, sometime in history, the developmental program leading to formation of a leaf must have been altered to generate a flower. There probably also exists an overall robust framework within which the floral diversity has been generated. A example of that is a gene called LEAFY (LFY), which is involved in flower development in Arabidopsis. The homologs of this gene are found in angiosperms as diverse as tomato, snapdragon, pea, maize and even gymnosperms. Interestingly, expression of Arabidopsis LFY in distant plants like poplar and citrus also results in flower-production in these plants. The LFY gene regulates the expression of some gene belonging to the MADS-box family. These genes, in turn, act as direct controllers of flower development.

Evolution of the MADS-box Family

The members of the MADS-box family of transcription factors play a very important and evolutionarily conserved role in flower development. According to the ABC Model of flower development, three zones - A, B and C - are generated within the developing flower primordium, by the action of some transcription factors, that are members of the MADS-box family. Among these, the functions of the B and C domain genes have been evolutionarily more conserved than the A domain gene. Many of these genes have arisen through gene duplications of ancestral members of this family. Quite a few of them show redundant functions.

The evolution of the MADS-box family has been extensively studied. These genes are present even in pteridophytes, but the spread and diversity is many times higher in angiosperms There appears to be quite a bit of pattern into how this family has evolved. Consider the evolution of the C-region gene AGAMOUS (AG). It is expressed in today's flowers in the stamens, and the carpel, which are reproductive organs. It's ancestor in gymnosperms also has the same expression pattern. Here, it is expressed in the strobili, an organ that produces pollens or ovules.

Similarly, the B-genes' (AP3 and PI) ancestors are expressed only in the male organs in gymnosperms. Their descendants in the modern angiosperms also are expressed only in the stamens, the male reproductive organ. Thus, the same, then-existing components were used by the plants in a novel manner to generate the first flower. This is a recurring pattern in evolution.

Factors Influencing Floral Diversity

How is the enormous diversity in the shape, color and sizes of flowers established? There is enormous variation in the developmental program in different plants. For example, monocots possess structures like lodicules and palea, that were believed to be analogous to the dicot petals and carpels respectively.It turns out that this is true, and the variation is due to slight changes in the MADS-box genes and their expression pattern in the monocots. Another example is that of a plant called Linaria vulgaris, which has two kinds of flower symmetries- radial and bilateral. These symmetries are due to epigenetic changes in just one gene called Cycloidea.

Arabidopsis has a gene called Agamous that plays an important role in defining how many petals and sepals and other organs are generated. Mutations in this gene give rise to the floral meristem obtaining an indeterminate fate, and many floral organs keep on getting produced. We have flowers like roses, carnations and morning glory, for example, that have very dense floral organs. These flowers have been selected by horticulturists since long for increased number of petals. Researchers have found that the morphology of these flowers is because of strong mutations in the Agamous homolog in these plants, which leads to them making a large number of petals and sepals. Several studies on diverse plants like petunia, tomato, Impatiens, maize etc have suggested that the enormous diversity of flowers is a result of small changes in genes controlling their development.

Some of these changes also cause changes in expression patterns of the developmental genes, resulting in different phenotypes. The Floral Genome Project looked at the EST data from various tissues of many flowering plants. The researchers confirmed that the ABC Model of flower development is not conserved across all angiosperms. Sometimes expression domains change, as in the case of many monocots, and also in some basal angiosperms like Amborella. Different models of flower development like the The fading boundaries model, or the Overlapping-boundaries model which propose non-rigid domains of expression, may explain these architectures. There is a possibility that from the basal to the modern angiosperms, the domains of floral architecture have gotten more and more fixed through evolution.

Flowering Time

Another floral feature that has been a subject of natural selection is flowering time. Some plants flower early in their life cycle, others require a period of vernalization before flowering. This decision is based on factors like temperature, light intensity, presence of pollinators and other environmental signals. We know that genes like CONSTANS (CO), FLC and FRIGIDA regulate integration of environmental signals into the pathway for flower development. Variations in these loci have been associated with flowering time variations between plants. For example, Arabidopsis thaliana ecotypes that grow in the cold, temperate regions require prolonged vernalization before they flower, while the tropical varieties, and the most common lab strains, don't. We now know that this variation is due to mutations in the FLC and FRIGIDA genes, rendering them non-functional.

Quite a few players in this process are conserved across all the plants studied. Sometimes though, despite genetic conservation, the mechanism of action turns out to be different. For example, rice is a short-day plant, while Arabidopsis is a long-day plant. Now, in both plants, the proteins CO and Flowering Locust (FT) are present. But in Arabidopsis, CO enhances FT production, while in rice, the CO homolog represses FT production, resulting in completely opposite downstream effects.

Theories of Flower Evolution

Theory was based upon the observation that a gymnospermic group Gnetales has a flower-like ovule. It has partially developed vessels as found in the angiosperms, and the megasporangium is covered by three envelopes, like the ovary structure of angiosperm flowers. However, many other lines of evidence show that Gnetales is not related to angiosperms.

Further Information: Anthophyta

The Mostly Male Theory has a more genetic basis. Proponents of this theory point out that the gymnosperms have two very similar copies of the gene LFY while angiosperms just one. Molecular clock analysis has shown that the other LFY paralog was lost in angiosperms around the same time as flower fossils become abundant, suggesting that this event might have led to floral evolution. According to this theory, loss of one of the LFY paralog led to flowers that were more male, with the ovules being expressed ectopically. These ovules initially performed the function of attracting pollinators, but sometime later, may have been integrated into the core flower.

One theory also suggests that humans have been one of the reasons for the diversity of flowers. This theory suggests that since the early settlers found flowers beautiful, they may have started selecting for them artificially. The flowers may have evolved to exploit the ecological niche being opened because of humans finding them attractive. The validity of this theory, however, is debatable, not least because flowers started diversifying long before they came into contact with humans.

Evolution of Secondary Metabolism

Many secondary metabolites have complex structuresAlthough we know a lot of secondary metabolites produced by plants, the extent of the same is still unfathomable. Secondary metabolites are essentially low molecular weight compounds, sometimes having complex structures. They function in processes as diverse as immunity, anti-herbivory, pollinator attraction, communication between plants, maintaining symbiotic associations with soil flora, enhancing the rate of fertilization etc, and hence are significant from the evo-devo perspective. The structural and functional diversity of these secondary metabolites across the plant kingdom is so huge that it is estimated that hundreds of thousands of enzymes might be involved in this process in the entire of the plant kingdom, with about 15-25% of the coding genome coding for these enzymes. Despite this, every species has its unique arsenal of secondary metabolites. Many of these metabolites are of enormous medical significance to humans.

What is the purpose of having so many secondary metabolites being produced, with a significant chunk of the metabolome devoted to this activity? It is hypothesized that most of these chemicals help in generating immunity, and in consequence, the diversity of these metabolites is a result of a constant war between plants and their parasites. There is evidence that this may be true in many cases. The big question here is the reproductive cost involved in maintaining such an impressive inventory. Various models have been suggested that probe into this aspect of the question, but a consensus on the extent of the cost is lacking We still cannot predict whether a plant with more secondary metabolites would be better-off than other plants in its vicinity.

Secondary metabolite production seems to have arose quite early during evolution. Even bacteria possess the ability to make these compounds. But they assume more significant roles in life from fungi onwards to plants. In plants they seem to have spread out using different mechanisms like gene duplications, evolution of novel genes etc. Furthermore, studies have shown that diversity in some of these compounds may be positively selected for.

Although the role of novel gene evolution in the evolution of secondary metabolism cannot be denied, there are several examples where new metabolites have been formed by small changes in the reaction. For example, cyanogen glycosides have been proposed to have evolved multiple times in different plant lineages. There are several such instances of convergent evolution. For example, we now know that enzymes for synthesis of limonene - a terpene - are more similar between angiosperms and gymnosperms than to their own terpene synthesis enzymes. This suggests independent evolution of the limonene biosynthetic pathway in these two lineages.

MECHANISMS AND PLAYERS IN EVOLUTION

The stem-loop secondary structure of a pre-microRNA from Brassica oleraceaWhile environmental factors are significantly responsible for evolutionary change, they act merely as agents for natural selection. Change is inherently brought about via phenomena at the genetic level - mutations, chromosomal rearrangements and epigenetic changes. While the general types of mutations hold true across the living world, in plants, some other mechanisms have been implicated as highly significant.

Polyploidy is a very common feature in plants. It is believed that at least half (and probably all) plants are or have been polyploids. Polyploidy leads to genome doubling, thus generating functional redundancy in most genes. The duplicated genes may attain new function, either by changes in expression pattern or changes in activity. Polyploidy and gene duplication are believed to be among the most powerful forces in evolution of plant form. It is not know though, why genome doubling is such a frequent process in plants. One probable reason is the production of large amounts of secondary metabolites in plant cells. Some of them might interfere in the normal process of chromosomal segregation, leading to polypoidy.

In comparison to animals, while the number of plant miRNA families are lesser than animals, the size of each family is much larger. The miRNA genes are also much more spread out in the genome than those in animals, where we find them clustered. It has been proposed that these miRNA families have expanded by duplications of chromosomal regions Many miRNA genes involved in regulation of plant development have been found to be quite conserved between plants studied.

Domestication of plants like maize, rice, barley, wheat etc has also been a significant driving force in their evolution. Some studies have tried to look at the origins of the maize plant and it turns out that maize is a domesticated derivative of a wild plant from Mexico called teosinte. Teosinte belongs to the genus Zea, just as maize, but bears very small inflorescence, 5-10 hard cobs and a highly branched and spread out stem.

Cauliflower: *Brassica oleracea* var botrytisInterestingly, crosses between a particular teosinte variety and maize yields fertile offsprings that are intermediate in phenotype between maize and teosinte. QTL analysis has also revealed some loci that when mutated in maize yield a teosinte-like stem or teosinte-like cobs. Molecular clock analysis of these genes estimates their origins to some 9000 years ago, well in accordance with other records of maize domestication. It is believed that a small group of farmers must have selected some maize-like natural mutant of teosinte some 9000 years ago in Mexico, and subjected it to continuous selection to yield the maize plant as we know today.

Another interesting case is that of cauliflower: The edible cauliflower is a domesticated version of the wild plant Brassica oleracea, which does not possess the dense undifferentiated inflorescence called the curd, that cauliflower possesses.

Cauliflower possesses a single mutation in a gene called CAL, controlling meristem differentiation into inflorescence. This causes the cells at the floral meristem to gain an undifferentiated identity, and instead of growing into a flower, they grow into a lump of undifferentiated cells. This mutation has been selected through domestication at least since the Greek empire.

EVOLUTIONARY HISTORY OF PLANTS

Plants have evolved through increasing levels of complexity, from the earliest algal mats, through bryophytes, lycopods, ferns and gymnosperms to the complex angiosperms of today. While the simple plants continue to thrive, especially in the environments in which they evolved, each new grade of organisation has eventually become more "successful" than its predecessors by most measures. Further, most cladistic analyses (although these are often at odds!) suggest that each "more complex" group arose from the most complex group at the time.

Evidence suggests that an algal scum formed on the land 1,200 million years ago, but it was not until the Ordovician period, around 500 million years ago, that land plants appeared. These began to diversify in the late Silurian period, around 420 million years ago, and the fruits of their diversification are displayed in remarkable detail in an early Devonian fossil assemblage known as the Rhynie chert. This chert preserved early plants in cellular detail, petrified in volcanic springs. By the middle of the Devonian period most of the features recognised in plants today are present, including roots, leaves and seeds. By the late Devonian, plants had reached a degree of sophistication that allowed them to form forests of tall trees. Evolutionary innovation continued after the Devonian period. Most plant groups were relatively unscathed by the Permo-Triassic extinction event, although the structures of communities changed. This may have set the scene for the evolution of flowering plants in the Triassic (~200 million years ago), which exploded the Cretaceous and Tertiary. The latest major group of plants to evolve were the grasses, which became important in the mid Tertiary, from around 40 million years ago. The grasses, as well as many other groups, evolved new mechanisms of metabolism to survive the low CO2 and warm, dry conditions of the tropics over the last 10 million years.

Colonisation of Land

Land plants evolved from chlorophyte algae, perhaps as early as 510 million years ago their closest living relatives are the charophytes, specifically Charales. Assuming that the Charales' habit has changed little since the divergence of lineages, this means that the land plants evolved from a branched, filamentous, haplontic alga, dwelling in shallow, fresh water, perhaps at the edge of desiccating pools.

Plants weren't the first photosynthesisers on land, though: consideration of weathering rates suggests that organisms were already living on the land 1200 million years ago. These organisms were probably small and simple, forming little more than an "algal scum".

The first evidence of plants on land comes from trilete spores from the mid-Ordovician (early Llanvirn, ~470 million years ago). The microstructure of the earliest spores resembles that of modern liverwort spores, suggesting they share an equivalent grade of organisation.

Trilete spores are the progeny of spore tetrads. These consist of four identical, connected spores, produced when a single cell undergoes meiosis. Spore tetrads are borne by all land plants, and some algae Depending exactly when the tetrad splits, each of the four spores may bear a "trilete mark", a Y-shape, reflecting the points at which each cell was squashed up against its neighbours However, in order for this to happen, the spore walls must be sturdy and resistant at an early stage. This resistance is closely associated with having a desiccation-resistant outer wall – a trait only of use when spores have to survive out of water. Indeed, even those embryophytes that have returned to the water lack a resistant wall, thus don't bear trilete marks A close examination of algal spores shows that none have trilete spores, either because their walls are not resistant enough, or in those rare cases where it is, the spores disperse before they are squashed enough to develop the mark, or don't fit into a tetrahedral tetrad.

The earliest megafossils of land plants were thalloid organisms, which dwelt in fluvial wetlands and are found to have covered most of an early Silurian flood plain. They could only survive when the land was waterlogged.

Once plants had reached the land, there were two approaches to desiccation. The bryophytes avoid it or give in to it, restricting their ranges to moist settings, or drying out and putting their metabolism "on hold" until more water arrives. Tracheophytes resist desiccation. They all bear a waterproof outer cuticle layer wherever they are exposed to air (as do some bryophytes), to reduce water loss – but since a total covering would cut them off from CO_2 in the atmosphere, they rapidly evolved stomata – small openings to allow gas exchange. Tracheophytes also developed vascular tissue to aid in the movement of water within the organisms , and moved away from a gametophyte dominated life cycle.

The establishment of a land-based flora permitted the accumulation of oxygen in the atmosphere as never before, as the new hordes of land plants pumped it out as a waste product. When this concentration rose above 13%, it permitted the possibility of wildfire. This is first recorded in the early Silurian fossil record by charcoalified plant fossils. Apart from a controversial gap in the Late Devonian, charcoal is present ever since.

Charcoalification is an important taphonomic mode. Wildfire drives off the volatile compounds, leaving only a shell of pure carbon. This is not a viable food source for herbivores or detritovores, so is prone to preservation; it is also robust, so can withstand pressure and display exquisite, sometimes sub-cellular, detail.

All multicellular plants have a life cycle comprising two phases (often confusingly referred to as "generations"). One is termed the gametophyte, has a single set of chromosomes (denoted 1n), and produces gametes (sperm and eggs). The other is termed the sporophyte, has paired chromosomes (denoted 2n), and produces spores. The two phases may be identical, or phenomenally different.

The overwhelming pattern in plant evolution is for a reduction of the gametophytic phase, and the increase in sporophyte dominance. The algal ancestors to land plants were almost certainly haplobiontic, being haploid for all their life cycles, with a unicellular zygote providing the 2n stage. All land plants (i.e. embryophytes) are diplobiontic – that is, both the haploid and diploid stages are multicellula

There are two competing theories to explain the appearance of a diplobiontic lifecycle.

The interpolation theory (also known as the antithetic or intercalary theory) holds that the sporophyte phase was a fundamentally new invention, caused by the mitotic division of a freshly germinated zygote, continuing until meiosis produces spores. This theory implies that the first sporophytes would bear a very different morphology to the gametophyte, on which they would have been dependent This seems to fit well with what we know of the bryophytes, in which a vegetative thalloid gametophyte is parasitised by simple sporophytes, which often comprise no more than a sporangium on a stalk. Increasing complexity of the ancestrally simple sporophyte, including the eventual acquisition of photosynthetic cells, would free it from its dependence on a sporophyte, as we see in some hornworts (Anthoceros), and eventually result in the sporophyte developing organs and vascular tissue, and becoming the dominant phase, as in the tracheophytes (vascular plants). This theory may be supported by observations that smaller Cooksonia individuals must have been supported by a gametophyte generation. The observed appearance of larger axial sizes, with room for photosynthetic tissue and thus self-sustainability, provides a possible route for the development of a self-sufficient sporophyte phase.

The alternative hypothesis is termed the transformation theory (or homologous theory). This posits that the sporophyte appeared suddenly by a delay in the occurrence of meiosis after the zygote germinated. Since the same genetic material would be employed, the haploid and diploid phases would look the same. This explains the behaviour of some algae, which produce alternating phases of identical sporophytes and gametophytes. Subsequent adaption to the desiccating land environment, which makes sexual reproduction difficult, would result in the simplification of the sexually active gametophyte. and elaboration of the sporophyte phase to better disperse the waterproof spores. The tissue of sporophytes and gametophytes preserved in the Rhynie chert is of similar complexity, which is taken to support this hypothesis.

Water Transport

In order to photosynthesise, plants must uptake CO_2 from the atmosphere. However, this comes at a price: while stomata are open to allow CO_2 to enter, water can evaporate. Water is lost much faster than CO_2 is absorbed, so plants need to replace it, and have developed systems to transport water from the moist soil to the site of photosynthesis. Early plants sucked water between the walls of their cells, then evolved the ability to control water loss (and CO_2 acquisition) through the use of stomata. Specialised water transport tissues soon evolved in the form of hydroids, tracheids, then secondary xylem, followed by an endodermis and ultimately vessels.

The high CO_2 levels of the Silu-Devonian, when early plants were colonising land, meant that the need for water was relatively low in the early days; as CO_2 was withdrawn from the atmosphere by plants, and stored in coal, so more water was lost in its capture, and more elegant transport mechanisms evolved. As water transport mechanisms, and waterproof cuticles, evolved, plants could survive without being continually covered by a film of water. This transition from poikilohydry to homoiohydry opened up new potential for colonisation. Plants were then faced with a balance, between transporting water as efficiently as possible and preventing transporting vessels to implode and cavitate.

During the Silurian, CO_2 was readily available, so little water needed expending to acquire it. By the end of the Carboniferous, when CO_2 levels had lowered to something approaching today's, around 17 times more water was lost per unit of CO_2 uptake However, even in these "easy" early days, water was at a premium, and had to be transported to parts of the plant from the wet soil to avoid desiccation. This early water transport took advantage of the cohesion-tension mechanism inherent in water. Water has a tendency to diffuse to areas that are drier, and this process is exacberated when water can be wicked along a fabric with small spaces. In small passages, such as that between the plant cell walls (or in tracheids), a column of water behaves like rubber – when molecules evaporate from one end, they literally pull the molecules behind them along the channels. Therefore transpiration alone provided the driving force for water transport in early plants However, without dedicated transport vessels, the cohesion-tension mechanism cannot transport water more than about 2cm, severely limiting the size of the earliest plants. This process demands a steady supply of water from one end, to maintain the chains; to avoid exhausing it, plants developed a waterproof cuticle. Early cuticle may not have had pores but did not cover the entire plant surface, so that gas exchange could continue. However, dehydration at times was inevitable; early plants cope with this by having a lot of water stored between their cell walls, and when it comes to it sticking out the tough times by putting life "on hold" until more water is supplied.

In order to be free from the constraints of small size and constant moisture that the parenchymatic transport system inflicted, plants needed a more efficient water transport system.

During the early Silurian, they developed specialized cells, which were lignified (or bore similar chemical compounds) to avoid implosion; this process coincided with cell death, allowing their innards to be emptied and water to be passed through them. These wider, dead, empty cells were a million times more conductive than the inter-cell method, giving the potential for transport over longer distances, and higher CO_2 diffusion rates.

The first macrofossils to bear water-transport tubes *in situ* are the early Devonian pretracheophytes Aglaophyton and Horneophyton, which have structures very similar to the hydroids of modern mosses. Plants continued to innovate new ways of reducing the resistance to flow within their cells, thereby increasing the efficiency of their water transport. Bands on the walls of tubes, in fact apparent from the early Silurian onwards are an early improvisation to aid the easy flow of water Banded tubes, as well as tubes with pitted ornamentation on their walls, were lignified and, when they form single celled conduits, are considered to be tracheids. These, the "next generation" of transport cell design, have a more rigid structure than hydroids, allowing them to cope with higher levels of water pressure. Tracheids may have a single evolutionary origin, possibly within the hornworts, uniting all tracheophytes (but they may have evolved more than once).

Water transport requires regulation, and dynamic control is provided by stomata by adjusting the amount of gas exchange, they can restrict the amount of water lost through transpiration. This is an important role where water supply is not constant, and indeed stomata appear to have evolved before tracheids, being present in the non-vascular hornworts.

An endodermis probably evolved during the Silu-Devonian, but the first fossil evidence for such a structure is Carboniferous. This structure in the roots covers the water transport tissue and regulates ion exchange (and prevents unwanted pathogens etc. from entering the water transport system). The endodermis can also provide an upwards pressure, forcing water out of the roots when transpiration is not enough of a driver.

Once plants had evolved this level of controlled water transport, they were truly homoiohydric, able to extract water from their environment through root-like organs rather than relying on a film of surface moisture, enabling them to grow to much greater size. As a result of their independence from their surroundings, they lost their ability to survive desiccation – a costly trait to retain.

During the Devonian, maximum xylem diameter increased with time, with the minimum diameter remaining pretty constant. By the middle Devonian, the tracheid diameter of some plant lineages had plateaued. Wider tracheids allow water to be transported faster, but the overall transport rate depends also on the overall cross-sectional area of the xylem bundle itself. The increase in vascular bundle thickness further seems to correlate with the width of plant axes, and plant height; it is also closely related to the appearance of leaves and increased stomatal density, both of which would increase the demand for water.

While wider tracheids with robust walls make it possible to achieve higher water transport pressures, this increases the problem of cavitation. Cavitation occurs when a bubble of air forms within a vessel, breaking the bonds between chains of water molecules and preventing them from pulling more water up with their cohesive tension. A tracheid, once cavitated, cannot have its embolism removed and return to service (except in a few advanced angiosperms which have developed a mechanism of doing so). Therefore it is well worth plants' while to avoid cavitation occurring. For this reason, pits in tracheid walls have very small diameters, to prevent air entering and allowing bubbles to nucleate Freeze-thaw cycles are a major cause of cavitation. Damage to a tracheid's wall almost inevitably leads to air leaking in and cavitation, hence the importance of many tracheids working in parallel.

Cavitation is hard to avoid, but once it has occurred plants have a range of mechanisms to contain the damage Small pits link adjacent conduits to allow fluid to flow between them, but not air – although ironically these pits, which prevent the spread of embolisms, are also a major cause of them These pitted surfaces further reduce the flow of water through the xylem by as much as 30%. Conifers, by the Jurassic, developed an ingenious improvement, using valve-like structures to isolate cavitated elements. These torus-margo structures have a blob floating in the middle of a donut; when one side depressurises the blob is sucked into the torus and blocks further flow. Other plants simply accept cavitation; for instance, oaks grow a ring of wide vessels at the start of each spring, none of which survive the winter frosts. Maples use root pressure each spring to force sap upwards from the roots, squeezing out any air bubbles.

Growing to height also employed another trait of tracheids – the support offered by their lignified walls. Defunct tracheids were retained to form a strong, woody stem, produced in most instances by a secondary xylem. However, in early plants, tracheids were too mechanically vulnerable, and retained a central position, with a layer of tough sclerenchyma on the outer rim of the stems Even when tracheids do take a structural role, they are supported by sclerenchymatic tissue.

Tracheids end with walls, which impose a great deal of resistance on flow; vessel members have perforated end walls, and are arranged in series to operate as if they were one continuous vessel. The function of end walls, which were the default state in the Devonian, was probably to avoid embolisms. An embolism is where an air bubble is created in a tracheid. This may happen as a result of freezing, or by gases dissolving out of solution. Once an embolism is formed, it usually cannot be removed; the affected cell cannot pull water up, and is rendered useless.

End walls excluded, the tracheids of prevascular plants were able to operate under the same hydraulic conductivity as those of the first vascular plant, Cooksonia.

The size of tracheids is limited as they comprise a single cell; this limits their length, which in turn limits their maximum useful diameter to 80 µm. Conductivity grows with the fourth power of diameter, so increased diameter has huge rewards; vessel elements, consisting of a number of cells, joined at their ends, overcame this limit and allowed larger tubes to form, reaching diameters of up to 500 µm, and lengths of up to 10 m.

Vessels first evolved during the dry, low CO_2 periods of the late Permian, in the horsetails, ferns and Selaginellales independently, and later appeared in the mid Cretaceous in angiosperms and gnetophytes. Vessels allow the same cross-sectional area of wood to transport around a hundred times more water than tracheids! This allowed plants to fill more of their stems with structural fibres, and also opened a new niche to vines, which could transport water without being as thick as the tree they grew on Despite these advantages, tracheid-based wood is a lot lighter, thus cheaper to make, as vessels need to be much more reinforced to avoid cavitation.

EVOLUTION OF LEAVES

Leaves today are, in almost all instances, an adaptation to increase the amount of sunlight that can be captured for photosynthesis. Leaves certainly evolved more than once, and probably originated as spiny outgrowths to protect early plants from herbivory.

The rhyniophytes of the Rhynie chert comprised nothing more than slender, unornamented axes. The early to middle Devonian trimerophytes, therefore, are the first evidence we have of anything that could be considered leafy. This group of vascular plants are recognisable by their masses of terminal sporangia, which adorn the ends of axes which may bifurcate or trifurcate Some organisms, such as Psilophyton, bore enations. These are small, spiny outgrowths of the stem, lacking their own vascular supply.

Around the same time, the zosterophyllophytes were becoming important. This group is recognisable by their kidney-shaped sporangia, which grew on short lateral branches close to the main axes. They sometimes branched in a distinctive H-shape The majority of this group bore pronounced spines on their axes. However, none of these had a vascular trace, and the first evidence of vascularised enations occurs in the Rhynie genus Asteroxylon. The spines of Asteroxylon had a primitive vasuclar supply – at the very least, leaf traces could be seen departing from the central protostele towards each individual "leaf". A fossil known as Baragwanathia appears in the fossil record slightly earlier, in the late Silurian.[In this organism, these leaf traces continue into the leaf to form their mid-vein. One theory, the "enation theory", holds that the leaves developed by outgrowths of the protostele connecting with existing enations, but it is also possible that microphylls evolved by a branching axis forming "webbing".

Asteroxylon and Baragwanathia are widely regarded as primitive lycopods The lycopods are still extant today, familiar as the quillwort Isoetes and the club mosses. Lycopods bear distinctive microphylls – leaves with a single vascular trace. Microphylls could grow to some size – the Lepidodendrales boasted microphylls over a meter in length – but almost all just bear the one vascular bundle. (An exception is the branching Selaginella.)

The branching pattern of megaphyll veins may belie their origin as webbed, dichotomising branches.The more familiar leaves, megaphylls, are thought to have separate origins – indeed, they appeared four times independently, in the ferns, horsetails, progymnosperms, and seed plants. They appear to have originated from dichotomising branches, which first overlapped (or "overtopped") one another, and eventually developed "webbing" and evolved into gradually more leaf-like structures. So megaphylls, by this "teleome theory", are composed of a group of webbed branches – hence the "leaf gap" left where the leaf's vascular bundle leaves that of the main branch resembles two axes splitting. In each of the four groups to evolve megaphylls, their leaves first evolved during the late Devonian to early Carboniferous, diversifying rapidly until the designs settled down in the mid Carboniferous.

The cessation of further diversification can be attributed to developmental constraints, but why did it take so long for leaves to evolve in the first place? Plants had been on the land for at least 50 million years before megaphylls became significant. However, small, rare mesophylls are known from the early Devonian genus Eophyllophyton – so development could not have been a barrier to their appearance. The best explanation so far incorporates observations that atmospheric CO_2 was declining rapidly during this time – falling by around 90% during the

Devonian. This corresponded with an increase in stomatal density by 100 times. Stomata allow water to evaporate from leaves, which causes them to curve. It appears that the low stomatal density in the early Devonian meant that evaporation was limited, and leaves would overheat if they grew to any size. The stomatal density could not increase, as the primitive steles and limited root systems would not be able to supply water quickly enough to match the rate of transpiration.

Clearly, leaves are not always beneficial, as illustrated by the frequent occurrence of secondary loss of leaves, famously exemplified by cacti and the "whisk fern" Psilotum.

Secondary evolution can also disguise the true evolutionary origin of some leaves. Some genera of ferns display complex leaves which are attached to the pseudostele by an outgrowth of the vascular bundle, leaving no leaf gap Further, horsetail (Equisetum) leaves bear only a single vein, and appear for all the world to be microphyllous; however, in the light of the fossil record and molecular evidence, we conclude that their forbears bore leaves with complex venation, and the current state is a result of secondary simplification.

Deciduous trees deal with another disadvantage to having leaves. The popular belief that plants shed their leaves when the days get too short is misguided; evergreens prospered in the Arctic circle during the most recent greenhouse earth. The generally accepted reason for shedding leaves during winter is to cope with the weather – the force of wind and weight of snow are much more comfortably weathered without leaves to increase surface area. Seasonal leaf loss has evolved independently several times and is exhibited in the ginkgoales, gymnosperms and angiosperms Leaf loss may also have arisen as a response to pressure from insects; it may have been less costly to lose leaves entirely during the winter or dry season than to continue investing resources in their repair.

Evolution of Trees

The early Devonian landscape was devoid of vegetation taller than waist height. Without the evolution of a robust vascular system, taller heights could not be obtained. There was, however, a constant evolutionary pressure to attain greater height. The most obvious advantage is the harvesting of more sunlight for photosynthesis – by overshadowing competitors – but a further advantage is present in spore distribution, as spores (and, later, seeds) can be blown greater distances if they start higher. This may be demonstrated by Prototaxites, thought to be a late Silurian fungus reaching eight metres in height.

In order to attain arborescence, early plants needed to develop woody tissue that would act as both support and water transport. To understand wood, we must know a little of vascular behaviour. The stele of plants undergoing "secondary growth" is surrounded by the vascular cambium, a ring of cells which produces more xylem (on the inside) and phloem (on the outside). Since xylem cells comprise dead, lignified tissue, subsequent rings of xylem are added to those already present, forming wood.

The first plants to develop this secondary growth, and a woody habit, were apparently the ferns, and as early as the middle Devonian one species, Wattieza, had already reached heights of 8 m and a tree-like habit.

Other clades did not take long to develop a tree-like stature; the late Devonian Archaeopteris, a precursor to gymnosperms which evolved from the trimerophytes reached 30 m in height. These progymnosperms were the first plants to develop true wood, grown from a bifacial cambium, of which the first appearance is in the mid Devonian Rellimia. True wood is only thought to have evolved once, giving rise to the concept of a "lignophyte" clade.

These Archaeopteris forests were soon supplemented by lycopods, in the form of lepidodendrales, which topped 50m in height and 2m across at the base. These lycopods rose to dominate late Devonian and Carboniferous coal deposits. Lepidodendrales differ from modern trees in exhibiting determinate growth: after building up a reserve of nutrients at a low height, the plants would "bolt" to a genetically determined height, branch at that level, spread their spores and die. They consisted of "cheap" wood to allow their rapid growth, with at least half of their stems comprising a pith-filled cavity. Their wood was also generated by a unifacial vascular cambium – it did not produce new phloem, meaning that the trunks could not grow wider over time

The horsetail Calamites was next on the scene, appearing in the Carboniferous. Unlike the modern horsetail Equisetum, Calamites had a unifacial vascular cambium, allowing them to develop wood and grow to heights in excess of 10 m. They also branched multiple times.

While the form of early trees was similar to that of today's, the groups containing all modern trees had yet to evolve.

The dominant groups today are the gymnosperms, which include the coniferous trees, and the angiosperms, which contain all fruiting and flowering trees. It was long thought that the angiosperms arose from within the gymnosperms, but recent molecular evidence suggests that their living representatives form two distinct groups It must be noted that the molecular data has yet to be fully reconciled with morphological data but it is becoming accepted that the morphological support for paraphyly is not especially strong This would lead to the conclusion that both groups arose from within the pteridosperms, probably as early as the Permian.

The angiosperms and their ancestors played a very small role until they diversified during the Cretaceous. They started out as small, damp-loving organisms in the understory, and have been diversifying ever since the mid Cretaceous, to become the dominant member of non-boreal forests today.

EVOLUTION OF ROOTS

Roots are important to plants for two main reasons: Firstly, they provide anchorage to the substrate; more importantly, they provide a source of water and nutrients from the soil. Roots allowed plants to grow taller and faster.

The onset of roots also had effects on a global scale. By disturbing the soil, and promoting its acidification (by taking up nutrients such as nitrate and phosphate, they enabled it to weather more deeply, promoting the draw-down of CO_2 with huge implications for climate These effects may have been so profound they led to a mass extinction.

But how and when did roots evolve in the first place? While there are traces of root-like impressions in fossil soils in the late Silurian, body fossils show the earliest plants to be devoid of roots. Many had tendrils which sprawled along or beneath the ground, with upright axes or thalli dotted here and there, and some even had non-photosynthetic subterranean branches which lacked stomata. The distinction between root and specialised branch is developmental; true roots follow a different developmental trajectory to stems. Further, roots differ in their branching pattern, and in possession of a root cap So while Silu-Devonian plants such as Rhynia and Horneophyton possessed the physiological equivalent of roots, roots – defined as organs differentiated from stems – did not arrive until later. Unfortunately, roots are rarely preserved in the fossil record, and our understanding of their evolutionary origin is sparse.

Rhizoids – small structures performing the same role as roots, usually a cell in diameter – probably evolved very early, perhaps even before plants colonised the land; they are recognised in the Characeae, an algal sister group to land plants. That said, rhizoids probably evolved more than once; the rhizines of lichens, for example, perform a similar role. Even some animals (Lamellibrachia) have root-like structures!

More advanced structures are common in the Rhynie chert, and many other fossils of comparable early Devonian age bear structures that look like, and acted like, roots. The rhyniophytes bore fine rhizoids, and the trimerophytes and herbaceous lycopods of the chert bore root-like structure penetrating a few centimetres into the soil. However, none of these fossils display all the features borne by modern roots. Roots and root-like structures became increasingly more common and deeper penetrating during the Devonian period, with lycopod trees forming roots around 20 cm long during the Eifelian and Givetian. These were joined by progymnosperms, which rooted up to about a metre deep, during the ensuing Frasnian stage. True gymnosperms and zygopterid ferns also formed shallow rooting systems during the Famennian period.

The rhizomorphs of the lycopods provide a slightly approach to rooting. They were equivalent to stems, with organs equivalent to leaves performing the role of rootlets. A similar construction is observed in the extant lycopod Isoetes, and this appears to be evidence that roots evolved independently at least twice, in the lycophytes and other plants.

A vascular system is indispensable to a rooted plants, as non-photosynthesising roots need a supply of sugars, and a vascular system is required to transport water and nutrients from the roots to the rest of the plant. These plants are little more advanced than their Silurian forbears, without a dedicated root system; however, the flat-lying axes can be clearly seen to have grwths similar to the rhizoids of bryophytes today.

By the mid-to-late Devonian, most groups of plants had independently developed a rooting system of some nature As roots became larger, they could support larger trees, and the soil was weathered to a greater depth This deeper weathering had effects not only on the aforementioned drawdown of CO_2, but also opened up new habitats for colonisation by fungi and animals.

Roots today have developed to the physical limits. They penetrate many [quantify] metres of soil to tap the water-table. The narrowest roots are a mere 40 μm in diameter, and could not physically transport water if they were any narrower. The earliest fossil roots recovered, by contrast, narrowed from 3 mm to under 700 μm in diameter; of course, taphonomy is the ultimate control of what thickness we can see.

Arbuscular Mycorrhizae

The efficiency of many plants' roots is increased via a symbiotic relationship with a fungal partner. The most common are arbuscular mycorrhizae (AM), literally "tree-like fungal roots". These comprise fungi which invade some root cells, filling the cell membrane with their hyphae. They feed on the plant's sugars, but return nutrients generated or extracted from the soil, which the plant would otherwise have no access to.

This symbiosis appears to have evolved early in plant history. The AM are found in all plant groups, and 80% of extant vascular plants, suggesting an early ancestry; a "plant" fungus symbiosis may even have been the step that enabled them to colonise the land, and indeed AM are abundant in the Rhynie chert; the association occurred even before there were true roots to colonise, and is has even been suggested that roots evolved in order to provide a more comfortable habitat for mycorrhizal fungi.

Evolution of Seeds

Early land plants reproduced in the fashion of ferns: spores germinated into small gametophytes, which produced sperm. These would swim across moist soils to find the female organs (archegonia) on the same or another gametophyte, where they would fuse with an ovule to produce an embryo, which would germinate into a sporophyte.

This mode of reproduction restricted early plants to damp environments, moist enough that the sperm could swim to their destination. Therefore, early land plants were constrained to the lowlands, near shores and streams. The development of heterospory freed them from this constraint.

Heterosporic organisms, as their name suggests, bear spores of two sizes – microspores and megaspores. These would germinate to form microgametophytes and megagametophytes, respectively. This system paved the way for seeds: taken to the extreme, the megasporangia could bear only a single megaspore tetrad, and to complete the transition to true seeds, three of the megaspores in the original tetrad could be aborted, leaving one megaspore per megasporangium.

The transition to seeds continued with this megaspore being "boxed in" to its sporangium while it germiates. Then, the megagametophyte is contained within a waterproof integuement, which forms the bulk of the seed. The microgametophyte – a pollen grain which has germinated from a microspore – is employed for dispersal, only releasing its desiccation-prone sperm when it reaches a receptive microgametophyte.

Lycopods go a fair way down the path to seeds without ever crossing the threshold. Fossil lycopod megaspores reaching 1 cm in diameter, and surrounded by vegetative tissue, are known – these even germinate into a megagametophyte in situ. However, they fall short of being seeds, since the nucellus, an inner spore-covering layer, does not completely enclose the spore. A very small slit remains, meaning that the seed is still exposed to the atmosphere. This has two consequences – firstly, it means it is not fully resistant to desiccation, and secondly, sperm do not have to "burrow" to access the archegonia of the megaspore.

The first "spermatophytes" (literally:seed plants) – that is, the first plants to bear true seeds – were progymnosperms called pteridosperms: literally, "seed ferns". They ranged from trees to small, rambling shrubs; like most early progymnosperms, they were woody plants with fern-like foliage. They all bore ovules, but no cones, fruit or similar. While it is difficult to track the early evolution of seeds, we can trace the lineage of the seed ferns from the simple trimerophytes through homosporous Aneruophytes.

This seed model is shared by basically all gymnosperms (literally: "naked seeds"), most of which encase their seeds in a woody or fleshy (the yew, for example) cone, but none of which fully enclose their seeds. The angiosperms ("vessel seeds") are the only group to fully enclose the seed, in a carpel.

The embryo, completely isolated from the external atmosphere and hence protected from desiccation, could survive some years of draught before germinating. Gymnosperm seeds from the late Carboniferous have been found to contain embryos, suggesting a lengthy gap between fertilisation and germination This period is associated with the entry into a greenhouse earth period, with an associated increase in aridity. This suggests that dormancy arose as a response to drier climatic conditions, where it became advantageous to wait for a moist period before germinating This evolutionary breakthrough appears to have opened a floodgate: previously inhospitable areas, such as dry mountain slopes, could now be tolerated, as were soon covered by trees.

Seeds offered further advantages to their bearers: they increased the success rate of fertilised gametophytes, and because a nutrient store could be "packaged" in with the embryo, the seeds could germinate rapidly in inhospitable environments, reaching a size where it could fend for itself more quickly For example, without an endosperm, seedlings growing in arid environments would not have the reserves to grow roots deep enough to reach the water table before they expired Likewise, seeds germinating in a gloomy understory require an additional reserve of energy to quickly grow high enough to capture sufficient light for self-sustenance A combination of these advantages gave seed plants the ecological edge over the previously dominant genus Archaeopteris, this increasing the biodiversity of early forests.

Index

R

S

T

U

V

W

❑❑❑